THE WORDSMITHS

Here are five scintillating interviews that capture the magic and the mystery of the world of the Contemporary Indian Writer.

U R Anantha Murthy

Bhupen Khakhar

Krishna Sobti

Mahasveta Devi

M T Vasudevan Nair

... offer insights into the art and craft of writing, share their hopes and fears, and reveal that unique creative urge which makes their work what it is.

Also featured in this volume, the first in the series, is an alluring selection from their writing – fiction and nonfiction.

Essential reading for the browser and the bookworm!

Published by Katha, New Delhi

OTHER TITLES FROM KATHA

For Literary Connoisseurs

Katha Prize Stories, Volumes 1 – 5
Katha Classics*: Masti*
A Southern Harvest
Visions-Revisions

For Young Adults

A Unique Odyssey: The Story of the UN
YuvaKatha, Volumes 1 – 8

For Children

Tamasha! (a fun and development quarterly in English & Hindi)
Swapnasundari & the Magical Birds of Mithila
The Secrets of Kalindi: A Jigsaw Puzzle Mystery
HulGul ka Pitara: (A teaching/learning kit for Hindi)

Easy Readers for Women

Stree Ka Patra by Rabindranath Tagore
Paro Ki Kahani by Sughra Mehdi
Puraskar by Jaishankar Prasad
Thakavat by Gurbachan Singh Bhullar
Faisla by Maitreyi Pushpa
*Stree Katha (*a teaching/learning text in Gujarati, Hindi, Kannada, Malayalam, Telugu & Urdu)

THE WORDSMITHS

Edited by Meenakshi Sharma

KATHA
Rupa & Co.

First published in March 1996 by
KATHA
Building Centre, Sarai Kale Khan
Nizamuddin East, New Delhi 110 013
Phone: 4628227; 4628254; Fax: 4643998
e-mail: DELAAB05@giasdl01.vsnl.net.in

General Series Editor: Geeta Dharmarajan
Special Consultant: Keerti Ramachandra
Assistant Editor: Mridula Nath Chakraborty

Distributed by
RUPA & CO,
15 Bankim Chatterjee Street, Calcutta 700 070
P G Solanki Path, Lamington Road, Bombay 400 007
94, South Malaka, Allahabad 211 001
7/16 Ansari Road, Daryaganj, New Delhi 110 002

Typeset in 9.5 on 13pt Cheltenham by Suresh Sharma and Ramesh at Katha.
Printed at Saurabh Print-O-Pack, A/16, Sector IV, NOIDA.

ISBN 81-85586-48-9 (paperback) ISBN 81-85586-49-7 (hardback);

Contents

Acknowledgements

This book was put together with the help of many, many people. I wish I could acknowledge all my debts here. However, I would like to thank in particular –

- The Sahitya Akademi – for being the Katha Treasure Trove. We are specially grateful to Professor Indranath Choudhuri and Shri K Satchidanandan. And to Shri Lalit Kumar Jain, for all the the photographs he unearthed for us. Also Shri Sreenivasarao, Professor U R Anantha Murthy's Personal Secretary, and Shri Bhattacharya at the Library.
- Shrimati Dasgupta at the Lalit Kala Akademi.
- *Outlook* – especially Prashant Panjiar and S Rakshit, for their unstinting generosity in allowing us to use their transparencies and other material.
- Smita Mitra, for that invaluable, untraceable copy of the Mahasveta Devi commemorative issue of *Bartika*.
- Shri Trivedi, who translated at very short notice an essay we did not use ultimately.
- Shri Dharmarajan for his unfailing good humour and patience, and of course, for the innumerable icecream treats.
- Geeta, for believing that I could handle the project, and for shaping it – quite literally too! – from the disjointed mess I presented to her.
- Ganeshan, for his infectious enthusiasm and enterprise in arranging for our book to look special, to have that special touch.
- Taposhi, Ramesh and Ajith, for their invaluable input.
- Keerti and Jayeeta, Mridula and Suresh, for letting me take them for granted. And everyone else at Katha – a big thank you!
- The entire community of book lovers out there, who were the only inspiration for our attempting this book.

March 1996 Meenakshi Sharma

Introduction

Envy is a terrible feeling. Only, you can't envy what you have, says a sane voice inside me. I know I need not and I know Indian writers are ours to hold and cherish. But much of the genius of our country lies in regional literatures and, unable to read more than one or two of these languages or enjoy in the original the specialness of art and craft that each one of these languages fosters, it is difficult to step outside our self-deprecation and see our stories for what they are. When I manage to do this I – to take off from Anna Akhmatova – finally know what envy really is! Translations are but poor cousins that strive, oftentimes with a lack of faith in itself and its creations, to bring the best from this katha-khazana to readers who can't read the stories in their original language. And, even in reading translations, we feel the pride and pleasure of coming home to good fiction.

The genesis of this book lies in my deepfelt longing to know more about our writers and their writings, and the nonavailability of a book that satisfied this desire. I sincerely thank the five writers who are featured in this first volume of *Wordsmiths*, for giving Katha so much of themselves. Being self-analytical, going over tread ground, is difficult for all, and especially so for creative minds. We know this and we feel honoured to have what we have from these five wordsmiths.

The best of Indian writers have always empathized with men and women from nonliterate backgrounds, they who, unfortunately, still form a very large portion of our population. These people have a realization of ground realities that their counterparts from more affluent families often don't. But being nonliterate and having been given a colossal lack of confidence in their selves and in their thoughts, they have, till recently, discounted themselves, their idioms, thoughts,

---

The word, "wordsmith," came to mind serendipitously. I was gratified to find it listed in the *Random House Dictionary.* It means, An expert in the use of words.

language. URA and MT work, in one sense, like "insiders" though they do not come from non-literate families; so too does Bhupen Khakhar, in his own inimitable way. And women, though we have been writing for many centuries now, have let ourselves believe that we face a double handicap – being hesitant users of the written word and also being ignorant of the "real" world that writers write about. This is the disquietude that writers like Krishna Sobti and Mahasveta Devi put to rest, with stories that stand shoulder to shoulder with the best that men have written. Here, in their own words, we understand these writers and what drives them, more clearly.

Katha is a registered nonprofit organization whose objectives are twofold. To bring to a wider readership the best of Indian literature – both for the common reader and for neo-literate people – and through translations from one language to another, including English. The second objective is to develop suitable teaching/learning materials for children and women who are just starting out on the road to literacy, using the story for effective communication.

The making of T/L materials has, till now, focussed more on children, basically working children, neo-literates. But I find that many of us who have had our formal education in English are neo-literate when it comes to Indian literature. In 1995, Katha brought out the first of the Classics, *Masti Venkatesa Iyengar,* a well-researched book on that "grand old man" of Kannada literature. This was specifically seen for possible use in academia. This is a project we are proud of. *Wordsmiths,* we hope, will offer the same interest and enriching experience for readers and students alike.

We also hope that this and the other books of Katha Vilasam, the story research and resource centre of Katha, will add to efforts already on for a more sustained dialogue between the various languages that facilitates a deeper understanding of ourselves as Indians.

March 1996

Geeta Dharmarajan

For all serious daring starts from within.

– Eudora Welty

U.R. Ananthamurthy

U R ANANTHA MURTHY

"All of us, part child and part adult, prepare to face our own death with the magic of words through which we glimpse an immortality, that was given to us in our childhood."
– Anantha Murthy

Childhood, death, the magic of words, immortality – these words perhaps sum up the major preoccupations of this eminent Kannada writer. As an outstanding creative writer, critic, editor and teacher, U R Anantha Murthy has had a seminal impact on Kannada literature and culture in the last few decades and is one of the most charismatic Indian literary personalities living today.

It is difficult to imagine the benign-looking sixty-four-year-old Jnanpith Award winner as the fire-breathing iconoclastic college teacher of the '60s and '70s. A radical of the Lohiaite school, Anantha Murthy, in his own words, is a "critical insider." He writes about the delicate balance in perspective that is demanded by such a positioning of oneself, "As an insider, you are orthodox, blind to pitfalls. Because of the great continuity of Indian society, we tend to think that reality is rocklike; we were not like this earlier. Shankara, Gautam Buddha: they were all critical insiders. But the danger of being just critical is that one gets westernized, one falls out of sympathy, one can't see any of the dynamics of change." This constant struggle to balance contraries can be traced to a great extent to Anantha Murthy's upbringing.

Born into an orthodox vaidika brahmin family in Melige, a small village in the Tirthahalli taluka of Karnataka, Udipi Rajgopalacharya Anantha Murthy was named after Ananthapadmanabha, the famous deity of Kerala. His early education was acquired in Sanskrit at a traditional pathashala. But the brahmin boy, who "grew up with a fascination for the Sanyasi," was inducted into socialist ideology even while he was in school. He recalls how on a single day he would be "exposed to worldviews of different centuries and they coexisted in my mind." He contends that this bewildering coexistence of centuries in his being is also specifically a legacy of his father who walked a curious path between tradition and change.

"My father was full of contradictions. He was a self-taught man who managed to escape from his priesthood, passed many examinations privately, taught himself astrology, astronomy, and mathematics and got himself ultimately entangled in the intricacies of law for a livelihood ... He had a great wealth of English words in print, but not as a spoken language. He took more care that I learnt by heart Burke's speech impeaching Warren Hastings than the Purusha Sukta, a great hymn of the Vedas. This was an exercise he gave me to increase my vocabulary and I chanted the speech exactly like a mantra. How absurd I should have looked then! – sitting cross-legged in an agrahara on the bank of a river."

Anantha Murthy's journey, which began at a pathashala veered

"All of us ..." is taken from U R Anantha Murthy's "Being a Writer in India," an unpublished talk delivered at the University of Iowa in 1986.

towards Maharajah's College in Mysore where he studied English for his BA. Though his first anthology of short stories appeared in print before he had completed his MA, he found his sentimental-progressive literary practice challenged by writer-friends in the Mysore college where he went for his master's. M Gopalakrishna Adiga, Ramachandra Sharma, Shantinath Desai, Yashawant Chittal and P Lankesh – all were part of the intellectual circle in which Anantha Murthy explored his literary ideas and reconsidered his ideological position. From such an exchange was born the Navya movement, an experiment in Modernist writing that went on to transform the Kannada literary scene.

In 1956, *Samskara* shook the Kannada-reading world. There has been no looking back since. Each work of his is a milestone in Kannada literature – perhaps the reason behind the considerable critical acclaim he has achieved in spite of a not very substantial body of work.

D R Nagaraj, the eminent Kannada critic, distinguishes Anantha Murthy's literary output into two phases. In the first, or the "radical" phase he is preoccupied with charting out the making of rebels in society. His heroes of this phase – Praneshacharya, Ranga and Jagannatha – seek personal freedom by flouting the taboos of a caste-ridden society. The second or "self-reflexive" phase of Anantha Murthy's career finds its first expression in "Suryanakudure," a classic of contemporary writing in Kannada. This phase is characterized by self-doubt and, particularly, by the critical examination of his earlier "radical" values.

For Anantha Murthy, ideological rethinking seems to work in life too. Thus the rebellious act of marrying a Protestant Christian woman which led to a breach in relationship with his father. Also the observance of rites like grihapravesh and pindadaan in an otherwise iconoclastic, socialist way of life.

In "The Dynamics of Textuality," Anantha Murthy writes, "It is our deepest desire to belong authentically to our community, which prompts us to both read and write, this way – for we want to renew ourselves in the naked truth of our experience and shed all falseness and dishonest acquiescence to the ideological imperatives of our communities." This desire to belong to one's community combined with an irresistible urge to explore, experiment with and reinvent society is the hallmark of Anantha Murthy's vision.

Three decades into an engagement with words and after scores of felicitations and citations, Anantha Murthy still maintains, "It is very important for a post-colonial writer to be subversive about many aspects of his society – both present and past." His works are primarily an enquiry into the nature of the self in a situation that dramatizes the contradictions and paradoxes of a society at a crucial phase of transformation. The individual, in his works, is a social entity whose strengths and failings reflect the contradictions of the historical moment of the society.

Besides being a novelist and a short-story writer, Anantha Murthy is also a playwright and a poet. In fact, he confesses to being "more like a poet working on fiction." Another favourite genre of his is the personal essay because it is "contemplative and neither a story nor a poem" – though he does seem to transform it into both!

In the course of a very distinguished academic career Anantha Murthy has received numerous fellowships and has lectured at institutions all over the world. Since 1993, he has been the president of the Sahitya Akademi. He also edits *Rujuvathu*, a journal in Kannnada, which aims to encourage "experimentation in creative writing and open-minded dialogues on disturbing socio-political and cultural questions." He lives with his family in Manipal, helping look after his grandchild.

Anantha Murthy once said, "I have my obsessions. All my stories are related to one another. You can be a writer only if your memory has a certain continuity. Everything I write is just one story." If that is so, we eagerly await more "versions" of The Story!

U R ANANTHA MURTHY

in conversation with
Prasanna

Anantha Murthy is a very articulate person. And he is a brahmin. He is also acutely aware of both these aspects of his identity. That is perhaps the reason why Anantha Murthy has emerged as the first Kannada writer to focus on the problem of brahminical caste hierarchy in a big way. I am not suggesting here that he always succeeds in crossing this brahminical barrier to articulation in his literary texts. But whenever he has, masterpieces of prose writing were produced in Kannada.

I am happy that my conversation with Anantha Murthy on the problem of articulation is being published along with the English translation of his short story "Mouni"(The Silent One). The silent man in "Mouni" is silent by choice. He is stating something by sealing his lips. And the mouni in Anantha Murthy's story is also a brahmin.

When Anantha Murthy insists in his innumerable and eloquent discourses all over the country – which are becoming one too many for the liking of some of us! – that shudras and women should speak up, he is actually voicing a profound concern of his. So, I asked him about his women. He agreed that they are not yet articulate in the real sense. But he challenged me by saying, "You wait and see!" I am waiting to see some women from Anantha Murthy's pen who go beyond Chandri, beyond Akkayya, and beyond Jaratkaru's mother. I have a feeling, it is the women who can lead Anantha Murthy beyond wherever he is at present.

***P:** It is a little difficult to talk to you because so much has been already discussed. I was wondering what to focus on. And it struck me that every writer is striving to become articulate. Sometimes writers strive all their lives. You are articulate in your public life and you are most articulate in your writings. Your characters – your men – are very intelligent and they have the desire to record their thoughts and experiences. They are a major group of characters in your works, people like Praneshacharya in* Samskara*. There are also some beautifully inarticulate people. The most inarticulate is Venkata in "Suryanakudure."*

AS A WRITER, I AM FASCINATED BY PEOPLE WHO ARE NOT ANALYTICAL.

We gratefully acknowledge the contribution of Lalita Vivekanand who also participated in this conversation with URA on October 9, 1995 at the Sahitya Akademi.

And your women are always inarticulate. The question is: When were you inarticulate?

URA: That is a difficult question to answer. My immediate response is that for those characters of mine who talk a lot, articulation itself is part of their problem. They are, in fact, really simple people who are not so articulate. I have done some explicit thinking on this. I have begun to realize that, particularly in Karnataka, there are two kinds of consciousness today, depending on the caste or social class to which one belongs. There is one type of family setup where people talk to each other. The father talks, the mother talks, children talk. They all say what is happening to them, they articulate their experiences. They usually belong to the upper classes or upper castes. But this does not happen in the lower castes. They are not analytical. As a writer, I am fascinated by people who are not analytical. People who are not so articulate are more metaphorical and people who are articulate are analytical. One of the important things about my work is that I am analytical as well as metaphorical, allegorical as well as realistic. Bringing these two aspects of my own being together is the problem I face.

P: *This actually takes us to the most obvious problematic: Caste. Fortunately in your writing, the articulate and the inarticulate do not automatically become the privileged and the handicapped. The inarticulate, as you say are metaphorical and the articulate are intellectual. Then it manifests itself at other levels. For example, the problem of literacy and nonliteracy. How do you understand this in the context of the "voiceless" sections of society – women and those belonging to the lower castes?*

URA: I've addressed this problem in one of my recent stories. In "Akkayya," you have a woman whose mind is not grown, who is like a dumb creature, a "jantu," or a goddess. And then you have Srinivas, who is so articulate while describing her. He lives in the West, and is very analytical. He may even get an American grant to do this. He is anti-West and gets money to air this fact! This is one of the ironies I've been able to put in this story. Akkayya is framed by Srinivas, but she is also framed by me, the narrator. And you can see her from my frame or Srinivas's frame or, with the trick of the eye, you can see her by herself. I have succeeded in my effort if you can see her in the frame of the articulate and the not-so-articulate *and* without the frame. It should be possible to see her by herself. I was not able to handle the issue so well in *Bharatipura.* I did try, though not consciously. There, I made the son of the priest stammer. He stammers. But the harijans there don't stammer, they don't talk at all. And I use the neuter gender for them.

***P:** So, not talking is not inarticulate, but stammering is.*

URA: Yes. In a way the inarticulate are powerful people. They are seen as the people who can demolish the world of the articulate. In *Bharatipura,* Joisa, who is completely articulate can talk on anything, with great authority, but it is his daughter-in-law who commits suicide.

***P:** And Maalera Putta – he is not articulate in an intellectual sense but is more like a story teller; rather than analyzing things he articulates the silence.*

URA: That is why I always think of framing such people. Something curious is happening to us today. Our analytical and conceptual articulation comes from the English language. But only our mother-tongue can provide us with metaphors that describe emotional states. All these regional languages are now developing a kind of artificial prose. There is nothing wrong in this but the living language is the language that is spoken in the streets. Otherwise Persian, English or Sanskrit would have been our language. This is what is happening now among the educated

... THE LIVING LANGUAGE IS THE LANGUAGE THAT IS SPOKEN IN THE STREETS.

elite. Kannada has been preserved by the nonliterates.. I write in that language, but my articulation, my analytical self, my ideational self, all these come from my familiarity with the English language.

***P:** Here I want to explore the text once again. It has something to do with your exposure to English. I think your inarticulate phase, if you have any, is in those stories where you are talking about your stay in England, where you cannot, for example, handle the Western code of sexuality, as in that lovely story, "Clip Joint," in which the protagonist goes with his professor friend to a night club.*

URA: There also, you know, the story actually starts when the protagonist remembers his uncle, Subanna Kaka. It happens in Soho where everything is out in the open, even the human body, and he goes seeking this, admiring the West for its rational, analytical nature. At that moment, he suddenly remembers this uncle who gave up everything and went away, being guided by the falling of a leaf. Our protagonist also lets a leaf fall, deciding that if it fell on the one side he would stay, but if it fell on the other, he would go. And the leaf dictates that he should go. This completely contradicts all that he admires, and is derived from his Kannada world.

***P:** Does it mean that the analytical is artificial even in prose?*

URA: Yes. But it is not a defect, I have to contain it in my prose otherwise I would be writing folklore in Kannada! This has to happen, if you want to use these Indian languages, which have been used for at least three hundred years or so only to express our emotions in our daily life and not our thoughts ... Let me remind you that the best analytical minds in Karnataka write in English. For example, M N Srinivas. In Bengal, Amartya Sen, Ashish Nandy write in English. Nobody uses our languages for conceptual thinking. They use it to express only lovely feelings and artistic expressions. I have attempted to use Kannada not only for that kind of emotional artistic expression, but also to express thoughts, especially conceptual thought. Hence a problem creeps into a story like "Clip Joint," which is not merely an emotional reaction to a Western situation.

Look at K V Puttappa. He sanskritized Kannada, used very convoluted sentences. It was because he was struggling to make Kannada a vehicle of conceptual thought. One of the first to do so. Bendre, D V Gundappa did it too in their own ways. So did V Seetharamaiah when he wrote a book on Economics. All these people tried to use Kannada as an expression of analytical thinking. I personally think that I belong to this tradition.

***P:** But you know what happens in your texts, I mean in your creative writings, is actually the opposite of what you wish would happen. For example, in* Samskara, *Praneshacharya, the articulate, is fascinated with Naranappa, who is inarticulate – not because of any inadequacy but because he is consciously and angrily inarticulate. We all know the ideological context of the novel. The articulate person fails. It is the inarticulate one who is successful.*

URA: I want to accept such an analysis; it fascinates me. Take "Ghatashraddha" – there is this woman who cannot articulate at all, because she is experiencing a new reality. She can feel it growing within her. The other is a child who is learning to articulate, but has not mastered language as yet. These two are bound through the common link of inarticulation and become really close. It is only society that can reason out every action and it emerges as the villain. In "Mouni," one of my favourite stories, what you are saying is worked out. The more successful Bhatta there, the one who can talk and talk nicely, as we say in Kannada, is perpetually splitting hairs. The silent one, through his silence, finally overpowers the more articulate one. Appanna Bhatta too becomes silent in the end and sits with Kuppanna Bhatta, a piece of cloth on his head, like we

LET ME REMIND YOU THAT THE BEST ANALYTICAL MINDS ... WRITE IN ENGLISH. NOBODY USES OUR LANGUAGES FOR CONCEPTUAL THINKING.

do when we mourn the dead, when we sit for a shraddhakriya. I think that a lot of rituals came into practice because death articulates without saying anything.

P: *Do you mean to say that words are converted into a non-language or a symbolic language?*

URA: Yes. I have dealt with this aspect again in "Akkayya." Here too I am not yet fully conscious of what I am doing. I am trying to grapple with a certain reality.

P: *I think Chandrashekhara Kambar, the Kannada poet, had raised this point during the informal gathering of friends felicitating you on your 50th year. He jocularly said, "The difference between me and Anantha Murthy is that, in* Samskara, *when you are eating a banana, you are thinking about how to eat a banana. I can't do that." He was referring to the union between Praneshacharya and Chandri in* Samskara, *which is conveyed through the metaphor of the plantains she feeds him with. I remember his saying, in the midst of a burst of laughter from the young crowd, that he as a shudra could have only done one thing at a time – first had the woman and then thought about the consequence.*

URA: *(Laughs)* If Kambar or anyone argues like that, it has a kind of universal validity. At the same time, we have to recognize the fact that any literature that is ambitious, that contains the conceptual in it, has to move in the direction in which Bendre, Puttappa and others were moving, and in which I too move. But while doing so, one should not lose the magic. This magic is in the not-so-articulate.

A classic example is in Shakespeare's *King Lear.* Goneril and Regan are vociferous in their claims and totally insincere. But look at Desdemona. She says nothing, and it is her silence that is most appealing. Shakespeare was the first great writer to use the rhetoric of silence. Another great example of that kind is found in twelfth-century Kannada literature, in Allama Prabhu's writings. When Allama meets Muktayakka, she is mourning the death of her brother, Ajagana. Allama says, "Do not weep. After all life is mortal." She says, "My brother, who observed the oath of silence all his life, hit his head against a door frame and uttered – Shiva Shiva! So his vow was broken. He thereby died. He uttered just one word and then couldn't bear to live any longer. You who are so articulate, who use so many words, what do you know of the truth, the authentic experience?" In this context, Allama uses a word which thrilled me when I came across it for the first time – Shabdasutaka. I have a feeling that at this point of their conversation, Allama almost stutters. In his later poems, all metaphorical exercises have the force of silence. Whenever he talks metaphorically, there is no Shabdasutaka. He becomes metaphorical to overcome this. In the analytical, there is a lot of Shabdasutaka and once you are aware of it, like I am now, you have a problem with words.

***P:** The vulgarity of articulation in our daily life, the endless information that is disseminated through newspapers, TV channels, those endless seminars – as a writer, and as an insider, how do you handle this?*

URA: We who write in a regional language are protected. If I had been writing in English, I'd have had one hell of a problem. All Indian writers, who write in the regional languages have access to the deep springs of life. Because our language is truly preserved there. Television and media cannot affect the Indian bhasha writer as much as it does English writers. People say that English is a universal language, an international language. That itself poses a problem for a creative writer.

I THINK, A LOT OF RITUALS CAME INTO PRACTICE BECAUSE DEATH ARTICULATES WITHOUT SAYING ANYTHING.

***LV:** You have been exploring this theme in*

Shabdasutaka : Death of meaning. It was coined by the 11th century Bhakti poets who were fighting shabda which is also mantra.

your recent writings. In "Akkayya," Srinivas speaks in English when he is analytical and shifts to Kannada when he is emotional. This makes him sound "awkward" and thereby "authentic," as you have put it. The narrator, who is trying to "frame" Srinivas along with Akkayya, is himself within this frame as well as outside it. He reaches a state, that our classicists call Sthithapragna. What interests me is where does your "self" come in? As a protagonist or as a commentator?

URA: That kind of maturity of vision was possible for our classical writers – we have lost it now. It is a highly stylized and formal way of expression; I am almost envious of this kind of writing. Take, for instance, Kalidasa's *Shakuntalam* – the poet is able to show love in its most immature as well as completely mature form. There is a perfect reconciliation, a certain calmness of mind, as Milton said, "after all passion is spent." A lot of modern literature is condemned to the lot of the tragic, the artificial and the inauthentic.

It seems Shri Aurobindo has said somewhere, when the overt soul begins to talk, language becomes a little bombastic. I don't know how to put it. The Stithapragna, I don't want to laugh at it. It is, as you know, the ideal we want to attain, but in our times, it has never been contained in our language, in our expressions.

P: *What you are saying is absolutely true, but that itself is a major problem for a writer. There is no archaic possible in life, but an attempt is made in every text to create it. Take, for example,* Bhava. *There is always a pull towards reaching the archaic situation in love.*

URA: You are right there, but I want to say, with a certain humility, that it is not possible for us to achieve such perfection of expression. The classical writers have achieved it with great dignity. That's why there is so much emotional disturbance in Shakespeare. K V Puttappa had once said, "This Shakespeare, why did he have to end with so many deaths in *King Lear*? Couldn't he have brought in a supernatural power?" Beautiful! I felt so challenged when I read it. I kept on saying, "Puttappa is wrong! Wrong!" But I am glad he said it. For he was responding not just as one writer to another, but like a true aspirer of the sublime, looking at another culture like this.

If you examine yourself purely from a psychological sense of curiosity, then it becomes something like case-history. I would rather look at everything from a cultural or philosophical point of view.

***P:** I think, only an Indian author has this privilege of looking at life from a cultural and philosophical point of view and not merely a psychological one. An European writer may not be as well equipped to do that, as he hardly has the cultural reserves to operate within.*

URA: Take the case of the Kannada Navya movement. It is different from the Modernist writings elsewhere. It came as a reaction to the Nehruvian age of idealism. Girish Karnad's *Tughlak* is a good example. Gopalakrishna Adiga's poetry too critiques that age. By making it a politico-cultural statement, rather than an individual's analysis of the self and the society.

Our new poetry has its origin in the vachanas of the twelfth century. Even now, our vachanas seem to be the most Modernist of all poetry. A rupaka in Kumaravyasa, who wrote in the sixteenth century, is similar to the most modern of the metaphoric search we find in Navya literature. Of course we have lost a few things. There has been a shift – the earlier novels were written, for example, from an omniscient point of view. That meant a certain formal economy, an aesthetic concentration, a different kind of reality.

> PEOPLE SAY THAT ENGLISH IS A UNIVERSAL LANGUAGE ... THAT ITSELF POSES A PROBLEM FOR A CREATIVE WRITER.

***P:** Where would you like to go from this point? Towards the transcendental? Your works of the last ten years, for example,* Awasthe, *the mystical "Awadhanigalu" indicate such a possibility.*

URA: One should always feel a little shy or embarrassed

talking about the transcendental. Particularly in our country. We talk about it so easily that we arrive without travelling. My writing is a reaction against just that. One should not arrive at it or seem to arrive at it without recording the entire spiritual struggle and hence I don't talk about it much.

But I have been disturbed by some experiences. One of the things that deeply moved me long ago was an essay called, "A Lesson in Yoga," by Lohia. He had been tortured in prison, and at times he lost all sense of the past and the future. He is in a state of timelessness. He is neither afraid nor anxious. He can only remember these words that his grandfather used to quote: Yoga Chittavrittinirodhaha.

I have always seen the spiritual in people who are intensely political, intensely in love, or intensely engaged with life. In such people, the ability – actually it is more of a compulsion – to withdraw, is heightened. I have explored this in my novel, *Bhava*. But it is quite a clumsy book I was not in complete possession of what I am saying there. All creativity is the capacity to listen to one's self. It is very difficult to listen to yourself. We get so cheated by our public image that we conveniently forget about our inner selves. I am committed to socialism, equality. But I've always been aware that this itself can be seen as a public image. You see, if there is danger in spirituality, there is danger in respectability also. There is danger in everything when it is used for articulation. It suffers from Shabdasutaka. How to articulate without Shabdasutaka is actually what we are searching for. And spirituality is one area where one should not.

P: *You have used a very interesting word, "clumsy," to describe your book. One needs a lot of courage to write a clumsy book. A book might be clumsy also because the writer is going through a transitional period. Do you feel that some things just can't be said or that they are best left unsaid ?*

URA: Then, where is the need to say such things? Problems sort themselves on their own. There is always a fear but you don't act in this fear, because next day you have to have your meals and you go on living. This is the most terrible thing that I see in Kafka or Dostoevsky.

It happens when somebody very close to you dies, and the entire edifice upon which human existence is built seems to be niradhara. So no one dares to talk about it. I have a feeling that the greatest of men, like Ramakrishna Paramahansa, Mahatma Gandhi, faced it and then came back to assert that life is worth living. Ultimately what matters is not being afraid to ask that question: Is it worth it after all?

***P:** So, in that sense you don't agree with Kafka, because he said what should not be said and recorded what should not be recorded.*

URA: Even in Kafka, you know, what really troubles me is that there is a lot of joy in the exercise of language, in the force of the narrative. What is it, after all, but a kind of life force? You are using a life force to say that life is meaningless. He probably realized it. He was using vitality to say that vitality is lifeless. Why should you do that? But that makes Kafka one of the most interesting writers ever. There are moments when Dostoevsky seems to touch the same point. But you see, they were Christian writers, Jewish writers, and by their own culture they were given to that kind of abyss. We call the abyss Shunya. Only in our philosophy, Shunya is a positive thing.

ONE SHOULD ALWAYS FEEL A LITTLE SHY TALKING ABOUT THE TRANSCENDENTAL. WE TALK ABOUT IT SO EASILY THAT WE ARRIVE WITHOUT TRAVELLING.

***P:** Can we jump from Kafka to Masti, a writer so completely different and so much at ease with his tradition. His women never transcend this tradition. His men never transgress, and when they do, it is contained within some kind of empathy or sympathy.*

URA: Masti's world includes transgression, includes violence, but to the extent that he can handle it. This kind of vision is possible only in our land. If there is a sixteen-year old girl, full of joy, and looking forward to life, would I have the courage to give her a set of Kafka's works? Or even Dostoevsky's? But I would happily give her a whole set of Masti. Why? Because he won't mislead her either. He doesn't tell her that everything is beautiful or that she should go on dreaming.

***P:** He is not a "Mysore Mallige."*

URA: No, no! He knows how difficult is the passage to adulthood and the inevitability of it. He gently makes one understand the need to accept life. He is not a liar who makes everything sweet. Yet he is not like Kafka or Dostoevsky. I am not saying that Masti is greater than either of these, but no European writer can write like Masti, without becoming dull or boring. Masti had the benefit of experiencing a continuous tradition, something that is peculiar to this country

***P:** Would you care to elaborate on that?*

URA: You see, the great thing about the West is their living culture, what they have built, what they have achieved. Their cultural progression has been unchristian, but their entire mental make-up has been influenced by Christianity. So there is a constant friction between their religion and their everyday existence. This tension has produced some of the best literature in the West. The kind of intensity you find in Tolstoy is possible because he believes in a religious truth which runs counter to the logical progression of his civilization. Similarly with Dostoevsky's *The Brothers Karamazov.* The Indian philosophical system is altogether different; it is all-inclusive. Prakritai Namaha Vikratai Namaha. Namaha to Prakriti, and to Vikrati as well. So our creativity has to be very different. Our entire philosophical system does not have any scope for an intensity born out of friction. Our intensity is that of Bhakti.

***P:** Where the sensuous becomes more abstract, where love becomes the ultimate, and nothing else.*

Mysore Mallige: A popular collection of lyrical Kannada songs on marriage and love, written by Narasimha Swamy. It was severely criticized by the Modernists.

URA: Yes. Nothing else, but Leela. It does not include tragedy. Leela is a way of including both Prakriti as well as Vikrati.

We have been brought up to think not to make a difference between man and women. There is a hermaphrodite area in Indian writing. Basava was like a woman, and so was Gandhiji. Surely there is something lacking in male writer who cannot also be a woman.

***L:** You were talking about the kind of intensity that is possible only in Bhakti. There the deity is Purusha and the devotee or bhakta is always Prakriti. This Prakriti-Purusha or woman-man dialectic has been the basis of most creative writing. But in your works, men and women live in worlds of their own. They do not seen to communicate with each other.*

***P:** To put it simply, you do not fight with your women. Why?*

URA: But I don't think I have ever made domestic happiness in marriage to be the only reality.

***P:** So they don't confront you, the women in* Samskara, *in "Ghattashraddha," the way they do Strindberg, for example.*

URA *(smiling)*: Well – wait for my next work ...

MOUNI

Translated by
H Y Sharada Prasad

Bhavikere Kuppanna Bhatta and Sebinakere Appanna Bhatta are like the cobra and the mongoose. Theirs is an old enmity, its origin lost to memory. Their houses stand on two hillocks half a mile apart. A fence in the valley separates their estates. Both of them are tenants of Narasimha, the deity of the Sri Matha. Years ago both of them had come here to work at the areca plantations, with just a copper tumbler each and not a coin between them. Now both have accounts in Gopala Kamti's grocery shop six miles away.

Kuppanna Bhatta is the older of the two. His face looks like a sour dried mango, his fifty odd years etched on it. There was a time, in fact till just two years ago, when he was known for his sharp tongue – its one lash was enough to split anything. His short, hairy frame has been shrinking with each passing day, but the way he carries himself has not changed at all. The same shining bald head, the same pudgy nose, that curved jaw heightening the resemblance to a mango. But the small eyes, fiery once, are now covered with a layer of ash. The banana stains on his dhoti and the dhotra thrown over his shoulder, like his debts, have stayed with him through the years. He still keeps a wad of tobacco tucked into one cheek. Earlier, when angered, he would wait with drawn lips until his adversary stopped, stride to a corner of the courtyard, spit out the tobacco, and return to utter something which was like a tight slap. The other man would be left speechless. And Kuppanna Bhatta would mix another little pellet of tobacco with lime in the palm of his hand and, transferring it into his mouth, lapse into a long silence. Nowadays, his face is like a locked door. If anyone tries to pick a quarrel with him, the closed expression on his face seems to say, "You and I have nothing to do with each other."

Appanna Bhatta, on the other hand, has always been popular. He is a man who gets along with everyone. Words slide off his tongue as smoothly as a strand of hair drawn through freshly-churned butter. Even the brahmins of Buklapura, the agrahara two miles away, are his friends. The more so because Kuppanna Bhatta has antagonized them. Appanna Bhatta keeps a good house and his estate is a pleasure to see. There are chrysanthemums at his doorstep, a canopy of coconut fronds shades his courtyard. Coloured mats are spread out for visitors and no one leaves his house without being offered a cup of coffee. A far cry from Kuppanna Bhatta's courtyard. Cowdung here, children's shit there, garbage and flies everywhere, and the leeches too ready to latch themselves on to the soft flesh between the toes. Appanna Bhatta often says, "Even the hut of Koraga the sweeper is better kept than this."

"Mouni" (The Silent One) was first published in Kannada in a collection of the same name; Akshara Prakashan, 1972. This translation was published in *Indian Horizons,* 1989.

Kuppanna Bhatta's arrears with Gopala Kamti have mounted from year to year. He must owe Kamti more than a thousand rupees. Everyone knows that a messenger from Gopala Kamti goes to Kuppanna Bhatta every few days to demand payment. Appanna Bhatta is very different. At the end of each year he clears his account to the last rupee. He is equally prompt in paying his dues to the Matha from which both Kuppanna Bhatta and he have leased their areca estates. Not a single nut does he withhold. Not only that, the agent of the Matha who comes to collect the dues is shown the utmost respect, and served a special meal with payasam.

As for Kuppanna Bhatta, he owes the Matha some five thousand rupees. Every year he is short of ten or twelve maunds of arecanut. The Matha authorities have warned him either to pay up or surrender his tenancy. The agent is also worried about the manner in which Kuppanna Bhatta has neglected the plantation. He has often said that the only way to save the areca palms is to hand the land over to Appanna Bhatta.

Before the swamiji of the Sri Matha went to Kashi, Appanna Bhatta had invited him over to his house. Humbly, he had made an offering of fifty silver rupee coins on a silver plate and prostrated himself at the holy feet.

Even Kuppanna Bhatta's own brother-in-law believed that if Kuppanna Bhatta was not popular, it was because of his own behaviour. Little wonder then that the brahmins of Buklapura nodded when Appanna Bhatta said, "I can understand his resenting my shadow. But what wrong have you people done to him? Could he not have performed the upanayana of his oldest son here and invited you all to the feast? Did he have to go all the way to Agumbe by bus and spend twice as much money in the temple there?" Then he continued in a soft voice, winking, "One should not stretch one's feet beyond one's bed, our elders have said. But, believe my words, this man has got some concealed wealth. Otherwise, how could he have afforded such a lavish show?"

Why does he sit so listlessly, wonders Kuppanna Bhatta's wife Gowramma, who is confined by asthma to a corner of the hall. Even after the evening birds have fallen silent, and the cows have come home and been milked, and daughter Bhagirathi has lit the lamp in the puja room, he has to be reminded three or four times to sit down to his evening prayers. In the past he had never allowed the children to light the kerosene lantern for fear that they would break the glass. Now the older son wipes the glass, lights the wick and places the lantern on the jagali.

Gowramma remembers ... Two years ago, her brother Subrahmanya had come to visit her. Hardly anyone comes to their house now. But never mind. At least one of her brothers is now a good farmer, earning enough to live a decent life. That makes her happy. But why wasn't her husband able to do this? Appanna Bhatta too had come here in search of his fortunes. He had done well and could even invite Swamiji of the Matha to his house! After the meal was over, Swamiji had sent a boy to fetch Kuppanna Bhatta. But how much should her husband tolerate? How could he step into his adversary's house, over a threshold he had not crossed for thirty years? Was it possible for him to stand there and be humiliated by Swamiji in front of Appanna Bhatta? So he had done something he had never done in his life. He had taken refuge in the kitchen and said to Bhagirathi, "Tell the boy I am not at home." Naturally Appanna Bhatta added to it when he narrated this to Swamiji.

It is all one's fate. Otherwise why would he be tied down to someone like her, an invalid, racked by asthma twenty days out of thirty? Across the fence, Appanna Bhatta's palms are laden with bunches of arecanut. Here, in her husband's plot, the nuts fall off the diseased trees. No labourer stays with him. They all go to the other estate. He has antagonized everyone. There is not a single two-legged creature in the entire region he has not quarrelled with. But he has never taken advantage of people. He does not know what deceit is and has never told a lie to save his skin. But what a temper! It is all in his stars. Just as it is in mine to suffer before I die. Fate. That's all.

What was I thinking about? Ah, Subrahmanya's visit. He had not been patronizing. In fact he had shown great deference. "Bhavayya," he said, "You have no friends here. I hear the Matha people too are asking you to hand over the land. Bhagirathi has come of age. How long can you keep a girl, who has shot up like a banana plant, in the house? When you approached those Tirthahalli people, Appanna Bhatta came in the way. He is always sharpening his knife ... I have no right to advise an elder. But frankly, this plantation does not seem to suit your horoscope. Give it up and come away with me. You know that I have some five hundred areca palms in Halasoor. You take care of as many as you wish to. I shall look after the rest."

No matter how humble and hesitant Subrahmanya was when he said all this, Kuppanna Bhatta would, like Parasurama, fly into a towering rage. "Wait till I am dead. After that you can look after your sister and her children. Until then, mind your business," he said harshly, dismissing Subrahmanya.

That was two years ago. Where was all that anger now? Since the bill collector saab from Kamti's shop and that rude man from the Matha had begun to pester him, he has become half his size.

Then one day, he who had never asked for anything, stood before his wife and said, "Will you give me your ornaments? I will return them to you in six months." That note of supplication in his voice drove a dagger through her heart. All she thought of was, Let my husband, my taali, the symbol of my marriage, be safe. She opened her box, and took out the jewels which had come to her at her wedding and which she had preserved for Bhagirathi's marriage – earrings, a four-strand necklace, a chain, a gold belt, an ornament for the hair. She gave them to him, taking care not to let him see the tears in her eyes. She made only one plea to God: "Protect my husband, and let Bhagirathi get married into a good home." She kept telling herself, "What do I need these ornaments for? His self-respect is more important." But who would look at a girl who had no gold? She had kept the ornaments only for that reason. Her own disease-racked frame had no use for them. Tormented by the change in her huband's manner she waited anxiously for Subrahmanya to visit them again. She could confide in him and lighten her grief.

Bhagirathi was in the kitchen trying to coax some flames from the damp firewood. Her mother could hear her coughing with the smoke in her lungs. A few minutes later, Bhagirathi came out, wiping the tears streaming down her sallow cheeks, her hair tousled. "Amma, there is nothing to make hooli with," she said. Gowramma told her, "Then make cucumber-seed saaru."

Why shouldn't her husband go to Halasoor? How long can he carry on here? Appanna Bhatta has been pursuing him like a Yamadootha. If he can build a bund to prevent his plantation from flooding, can't he build a fence to keep other people's cattle from straying in? Or at least chase them away? Why did he have them sent to the pound four miles away? Her husband had waited and waited for the cattle to come home, and when they didn't, he had trudged all the way to the pound, paid the fine and had them released. Appanna Bhatta surely has his eye on their plantation.

Ganapa, who was five and whose belly was swollen from disease, went weeping to his mother. "Give this child some of the water you have washed the rice in," she told Bhagirathi.

No one in the neighbourhood cares whether we are alive or dead. Not once has anybody given my daughter a string of flowers or asked her how she was. Suddenly, the memory of the jewellery brought forth all the tears she had held back when she had given it to her husband. A fit of coughing followed. Wheezing, gasping for every breath, she stared at the darkness in the house around her, too weak to move from her corner.

Kuppanna Bhatta had decided that if his wife demurred even a little he would not touch the jewels. But she had not said a word. She had just opened the box and given him the small bundle wrapped in silk and he was overwhelmed. "This is my last chance to get rid of my debts," he thought as he pledged them in the bank for two thousand and five hundred rupees. He vowed to redeem the jewels in six months and restore them to his wife.

Then Kuppanna Bhatta sought out the smaller cultivators, those who had only a hundred or two hundred areca palms, and advanced them twenty-five rupees a maund, with the promise that he would pay another twenty-five after the sale. Even Appanna Bhatta had never gone beyond forty-seven or forty-eight rupees a maund, and had never paid more than fifteen in advance. So the smaller growers agreed to go along with Kuppanna Bhatta, who was then able to transport a hundred maunds to the wholesale mandi at Shimoga. "When the price goes up a little, I will come and conclude the sale. Let me know how the market is," he told the traders.

All this infuriated Appanna Bhatta. His regular clients had been snatched away from him. He told the whole town that here was clear proof that his rival had come into money. Kuppanna Bhatta failed to pay the rent, but had enough for speculating on the market.

Meanwhile Kuppanna Bhatta made a careful calculation of his liabilities. He scrutinized all the figures he had noted in the margins of the panchanga. He owed five thousand rupees to the Matha, one thousand to Gopala Kamti, and three hundred for the medicines for his wife's treatment. There was the interest on the sum borrowed from the bank. And the money he needed for Bhagirathi's marriage. The first thing he had to do was to get the jewels back. He could pledge them again the following year.

Arecanut should sell at sixty this year. That would give him a clear thousand by way of profit. He would pay two hundred rupees to Kamti, fifty to the doctor, two hundred and fifty to the Matha agent. He would get the gold back with the remaining amount and use it as his reserve capital. A few more such careful transactions and he would be a free man. He took the cowries from his bag, laid them out and looked for the omens.

A fly flew up from the manure-pit and sat on his nose. Mango-gnats and mosquitoes hovered around his face. As it was summer, the courtyard was dry. Every whiff of breeze brought the smells of the cowshed. A withered jackfruit tree stood in one corner. The child with the malarial belly was defecating a few feet away, with a black cur near his feet. A grey dog dozed on the ash-heap.

Kuppanna Bhatta rose, scratching the spot on his foot where a mosquito had bitten him. He went out and brought a twig of tube cactus which he tied to a beam in the roof to attract mango-gnats.

Just then Bhagirathi came out with a pot of water and asked Ganapa, "Have you finished?" The black cur and the grey mongrel rushed to the spot vacated by Ganapa and Kuppanna Bhatta, disturbed by their barking, shouted, "Hacha, hacha," to chase them off.

From a corner of the room came the sound of wood being sawed. It was Gowramma's wheezing. "Give her some medicine, Bhagirathi," Kuppanna Bhatta told his daughter and began pacing up and down the jagali.

The tiles will have to be re-laid before the monsoon. Or the damp walls will crawl with hairy caterpillars. There are a hundred holes on the floor where the water has dripped from the roof. It is difficult to find a dry spot for the children to sleep. And the mildew, it is everywhere – on the mat, in the rice container, even under the box which contains the family deities. It does not grow on people's buttocks, yet. That's all.

The flies covered the octopus-like branches of the cactus, making its green turn black in no time. Kuppanna Bhatta stood there, looking out in front of him. There was nothing in the landscape to hold his attention. Paddy fields in front of the house and then the jungle. A hill in the distance. A cart-track cut across the jungle from left to right. Someone seemed to be walking along it. "Who is it?" shouted Kuppanna Bhatta. "It is me, Manja," said the man who was carrying a large load of dried branches, without slackening his pace. "Wait a moment. When will you come to our place to split the firewood?"

"After I have finished the work for Sebinakere Ayya," replied Manja, moving away.

Feeling utterly helpless, Kuppanna Bhatta picked up a knife and went into the garden to bring in some banana leaves. By the time he returned, the three older boys had come back from school, which was four miles away. Bhagirathi was waiting for the cattle. The sound of wood being sawn continued to be heard from Gowramma's corner. The medicine had had no effect. Ganapa sat in a corner, stuffing his mouth with dry avalakki and pieces of jaggery.

Arecanut that season went up to fifty-one, fifty-two, and, in a month, to fifty-five rupees a maund. Kuppanna Bhatta waited for it to touch sixty.

"Your money has gone down the drain," Appanna Bhatta mocked those who had sold their stock to his adversary. They in turn gave Kuppanna Bhatta a hard time. Every day, ten to twelve people came to his doorstep and demanded immediate payment. Making excuses and holding them off exhausted Kuppanna Bhatta. With abject humility, he pleaded with them to wait just a month more. But they would not listen. So he was compelled to go to Shimoga and raise a loan of two thousand and five hundred rupees at fifteen per cent interest on his stock. He paid his suppliers ten rupees per maund and promised to pay the remaining fifteen in a month's time.

Seeing all these transactions being made by his rival, Appanna Bhatta instigated Gopala Kamti and the agent of the Matha to demand a settlement of their dues. "This is the right time for it," he whispered to them.

Gopala Kamti's bill-collector turned up one day at Kuppanna Bhatta's house and planted himself on the jagali. No amount of pleading could move even a hair of his moustache. He shouted at the top of his voice that he would not stir until he had been paid at least five hundred rupees.

If Kuppanna Bhatta had been the weeping type he would have cried. As the bill-collector's voice rose, Gowramma's breathing became harder. Like a man in the grip of a nightmare, Kuppanna Bhatta seemed to be incapable of any movement. Whenever someone passed by the estate, the bill collector's voice became louder.

At last, Kuppanna Bhatta went in, opened his box and brought out four one-hundred rupee notes. The bill-collector saab took them, mounted his bicycle, and still muttering, rode off. On the way back, he met Appanna Bhatta, reported to him what had happened and was treated to a tumbler of coffee.

Hardly had the saab left, when the doctor's compounder presented himself. His peace was purchased with a hundred rupees. There were still thousand rupees left. The loan would have to be repaid now from out of the profit. It was all right, Kuppanna Bhatta reassured himself.

But early next morning, the agent of the Matha turned up. Kuppanna Bhatta laid out a seat for him and asked him if he would have some coffee. The agent refused it. "I have come to you even though there is a swelling on my leg. Anybody else would have treated you roughly. You do not show your face at the Matha on your own. Even when Swamiji sent for you from Appanna Bhatta's house, you did not come. He who deceives the Sri Matha Narasimha, will not prosper, Bhatta-re. You had better settle your debts," continued the agent, as he sat there fanning himself. He had come to know that Gopala Kamti had received four hundred rupees.

The more Kuppanna Bhatta pleaded, the angrier the agent became. "I will bring a search warrant and a notice of attachment tomorrow," he said, preparing to leave.

Kuppanna Bhatta resigned himself to the inevitable. He counted out eight hundred rupees and handed them over to the agent. "You must pay the remaining amount by the next date or else you will have to give up the plantation," he warned before he left. And he hurried off to Appanna Bhatta's house for his afternoon meal.

The next day some of those who had sold arecanut to Kuppanna Bhatta besieged him. "We are in financial difficulties, Bhatta-re. The rainy season is coming. We need to buy things for the house," they said. The whole world seemed to know that Kuppanna Bhatta had some money!

The price of arecanut did not rise beyond fifty-five. In fact it tumbled to fifty. In dismay Kuppanna Bhatta hastened to Shimoga by bus and sold off the stock. He paid back the short-term loan to the last rupee, including the interest. He also paid off his suppliers in full. Only the jewels remained in the bank.

❦

Just before the rains set in, Subrahmanya turned up in his bullock-cart and implored Kuppanna Bhatta to go with him. "Come with me, Bhavayya," he urged. "I will find a groom for Bhagirathi. Gowramma's health has deteriorated and Ganapa is as thin as a stick."

Turning to Gowramma, he said, "Akka, my wife is pregnant. If you and Bhagirathi come and stay with us for a few months, you will do me a favour. There is no one to take care of her. Bhagirathi will be of great help. I will look for a boy for her. Don't listen to your husband. Come with me to Halasoor ... Why did you give him all your gold, Akka? He is a selfish, stubborn man. He cares only about his pride, his self-respect. His wife and family mean nothing to him. Why has he not done well like the other areca growers, tell me? I just don't understand any of this."

Gowramma replied, "How can I leave him in this condition ..."

"I am asking you to come only for a few months, Akka. Till the confinement," Subrahmanya persisted.

Kuppanna Bhatta did not say yes, nor did he say no. "It's her wish," he told Subrahmanya and left it at that. He refused to go with them. "There is no one to look after the plantation," he said.

Gowramma was torn between anxiety for her husband and the pull of the home of her birth. But Bhagirathi's marriage had to be thought of. And without the gold to give as dowry, finding a husband for her had become more difficult.

Kuppanna Bhatta spent the whole of the monsoon alone, cooking his own kanji. Without his wife and her wheezing, the house seemed to be swallowed up by silence. As the rain poured down, Kuppanna Bhatta spent many nights awake, his eyes wide open. And he came to a decision. He would get the gold back from the bank. He did not want to be obliged to anyone.

Where Kuppanna Bhatta had expected a hundred maunds of nuts from his own plantation, the yield that year was only fifty. Swamiji was away in Kashi at that time. Kuppanna Bhatta wrote a letter, and with great humility, asked for leniency just this once. He undertook to hand back the land the following year.

He waited for fifteen days. There was no reply. If he waited any longer, Kamti's bill-collector and the agent would descend on him and carry away the crop. The ornaments in the bank would remain unredeemed.

The arecanut had to be moved to the market before the debtcollectors could lay their hands on it. If he allowed the ornaments to remain in the bank, the interest would mount and he would not see them again in this lifetime.

He went to the town to inquire whether there was any lorry bound for Shimoga. There was only one, it belonged to Gopala Kamti's relation. He struck a deal, thinking, whatever has to happen will happen.

The very next day, Kamti's bill-collector presented himself outside Kuppanna Bhatta's house. His heart sank. Whatever he tried to say was drowned in the bill-collector's ranting. The man insisted that Kamti had ordered him to come back with not a coin less than six hundred rupees, plus fifty rupees more by way of interest.

The argument was conducted at such a pitch that one of Appanna Bhatta's servants heard it and carried the news to his master. Appanna Bhatta yoked his bullocks to the cart and promptly proceeded to the Matha.

By the afternoon, Kamti's man, who had gone back to report to his master, returned with some gunny-bags and scales. "Sell us fifteen maunds of arecanuts at forty-five rupees a maund, then we will have to pay you twenty-five rupees," he said, taking the money from his pocket.

The selling price in Shimoga was fifty rupees. Besides, Kamti's weighing scales were adjusted, so he bought at one weight and sold at another. "Not possible," said Kuppanan Bhatta gruffly.

The bill-collector saab made bold to step into the house. To Kuppanna Bhatta, a Muslim crossing the threshold was the limit. He sprang towards the room in which the arecanut had been stored and shouted, "You will see me dead before you touch this door."

The man was taken aback at the outburst. Wiping his face with a towel, he sat down, the scales in front of him. "What can you do when grown men behave like children?" he muttered. Kuppanna Bhatta made no reply. He shook with emotion. His lips trembled. But he continued to sit outside the door, his arm stretched across it. The bill-collector just stared at him.

Fifteen or twenty minutes had passed by, when the sound of the bells of a bullock-cart were heard. Kuppanna Bhatta recognized it as the cart from the Matha. For a moment, his body went limp and he shut his eyes. But he quickly steadied himself. The agent of the Matha walked straight in, accompanied by the shanbogh – the village accountant – the Matha storekeeper, and a servant with another set of weighing scales. "What is going on here?" asked the agent loudly. Kamti's bill-collector told him.

"He is our tenant. God's dues will be paid first, the annual rent as well as arrears. The grocer's claim can only come later. Go tell your master that," the agent said to the bill-collector. But the saab was not so easily cowed. He said Kuppanna Bhatta had promised that Kamti's debt would be cleared first. This was not true. He also described how he had foiled Kuppanna Bhatta's plan to move the arecanuts secretly to Shimoga.

"So this is what you have fallen to, Kuppanna Bhatta? You think you can swallow and digest what belongs to Narasimha?" asked the agent contemptuously.

With a meekness he had never shown in all his life, Kuppanna Bhatta told him about the petition he had addressed to Swamiji at Kashi. He took his janewara between his thumb and forefinger and vowed that if he was given a reprieve this time, he would clear the dues the following year.

"Clear the dues, he says! With what face can you say it? You have money to speculate on the market, but you have no money to pay up what you owe God. You were arrogant enough to defy Swamiji and not come when he sent for you. You are eating his food, God's food! You don't bother to take care of the plantation. Look at the way you have kept this place. Thath! Anyone would think that it belonged to an outcaste! Anyway, this is Swamiji's order." He took a piece of paper from his pocket and read it out. It said that the estate should be taken away from Kuppanna Bhatta and entrusted to Appanna Bhatta for cultivation.

The shanbogh put on his reading glasses and added up Kuppanna

Bhatta's dues – unpaid rent, loan and interest – and pronounced, "Six thousand." The agent told the storekeeper, "Weigh the arecanuts kept in the room."

The storekeeper had recently been employed by the Matha, after having lost all his money through trading in buffaloes. He was a dark, hefty man, built like Bhima. As soon as he heard the agent's words, he scrambled up to impress him. "Move. Move ...," he bellowed.

"Hoi, fifteen maunds of it should go to Kamti." The bill-collector was persistent.

"Will you clear out of the way, or should we set you right?" the agent threatened the bill-collector, looking as if he would swallow him up. The bill-collector hurriedly climbed on to his bicycle and left unceremoniously wondering what excuse to give when his master scolded him.

Once again the store-keeper shouted, "Move out of the way," to Kuppanna Bhatta, who sat there, barring the door. "Before you touch one arecanut in this room, you will have to go over my dead body," said Kuppanna Bhatta, loudly and firmly.

The shanbogh and the storekeeper were speechless.

"What did you say?" the agent challenged.

"That you will see me dead before you get to the arecanuts," Kuppanna Bhatta replied, his whole body burning with the fire of his resolve.

"You, born a Brahmin and you are descending to this, Bhatta-re!" said the agent. The shanbogh put in his bit of advice. But Kuppanna Bhatta was unmoved.

"Very well, you will see what you are in for," the agent said, as he made ready to leave with his entourage. On the way he went to Appanna Bhatta's house, instructed him to keep an eye on Kuppanna Bhatta lest he move the arecanut at night, and went off without having any coffee.

Kuppanna Bhatta sat for a long time where he was, until his legs went dead under him. Late in the afternoon, he got up and stretched his limbs to make the blood flow in them again. He drew the latch across his front door, bathed, and boiled some kanji for himself. When the cows came back a couple of hours later, he tied them up in the shed, gave them bran-water and milked them. He lit the lantern and sat down in the courtyard. He did not feel like cooking, so he warmed some milk, drank it and lay down right there. But sleep eluded him. After a long time he opened the door and went out. From the clearing in front of the house, he looked up at the sky. Through the still silence of the trees, he could see the silver of pre-dawn spread across the sky. He calculated the hour, then went back into the house, bolting the door behind him. His eyelids drooped with weariness.

It was only when the young cowherd called his name that he woke up. After the cows were led away, he drew water from the well and poured it over his head. He put a vessel of water on to boil.

Soon he heard someone pounding on the door.

"Bhatta-re, it is me, the ameen. Open the door."

Kuppanna Bhatta made no reply to the bailiff. He went and sat at the threshold of the room where the arecanuts had been stored. After a while, there was the sound of a bicycle bell. Then came the voice of Kamti, "Open the door, Bhatta-re. I shall pay you forty-seven per maund. You can clear my account." Kuppanna Bhatta did not move.

Kamti's bill-collector shouted, "Will you open the door or not?"

An altercation between the ameen and Kamti ensued. The ameen hurried away, threatening to summon the agent of the Matha.

Again Kamti said, "Bhatta-re, open the door. I will pay you fifty rupees. Settle my account."

When there was no answer even to this, he let out a volley of abuse. "If I had known what kind of a shameless man you are, I would never have let you set foot in my shop!" he said.

Then he ordered his bill-collector in a loud voice, "Budan, go to this man's brother-in-law in Halasoor and demand a settlement of our accounts. Do not move from there until you are paid the money. He cannot be as shameless as this man is."

Just then the agent arrived. He and Kamti began to quarrel. They sounded like raucous crows that gather around the rice balls offered to them during a shraddha.

The agent used his ultimate weapon. He told the town-crier, "Go and announce to the whole of Buklapura that Kuppanna Bhatta's movable property is going to be publicly sold."

The man began his job right there. Kamti's protests were drowned in that noise. Gradually, the drumbeats moved farther away.

"I will go to court," threatened Kamti.

"Why don't you," replied the agent.

The sound of the town-crier's drum faded into the forest. Silence descended on Kuppanna Bhatta's house. Outside, the noonday sun blazed.

"You have to take the next step now," the agent told the ameen. "Do whatever is necessary. The storekeeper will help you. If Kuppanna Bhatta gives any trouble, send for me. I shall be at Appanna Bhatta's place," he added, before he left.

"Bhatta-re, for the last time, will you open the door, or do you want us to break it?" the storekeeper called out.

There was no answer. He picked up a crowbar and rammed the door with it. The bolt rattled.

"Open the door now at least."

There was still no response. One more blow and the door flew open. Like a Yamadootha, the ameen stood in front of Kuppanna Bhatta who looked as if he was deep in meditation. The ameen signalled him to get up but Kuppanna Bhatta remained sittting, his eyes closed.

The storekeeper picked up Kuppanna Bhatta's shrunken body as if it were a handful of sticks and put him down outside, in the hot sun. One by one, he piled up the arecanut sacks in another corner of the courtyard. He was in high spirits. "Are the vessels and other things to be sold too?"

The ameen pulled out a piece of paper from his pocket and read out the order, "Everything movable and immovable is to be sold."

The storekeeper darted into the kitchen. He brought the milk vessel into the courtyard and poured out the milk on the ground. Then he brought all the goods out. A copper handai, a set of rice vessels, kadais, a set of bronze thalis, a silver jug, a copper teertha vesssel (the same one that Kuppanna Bhatta had brought with him from the plains), a sankha and a brass thali used for the puja, a number of tubs for storing water at feasts, a cradle, a collection of ladles, a torn mat and a patched blanket, a wooden bench, a dozen wooden planks, a framed silver picture of Krishna, a silk dhoti, a pair of brooms – everything except the holy box containing the family deity, the Saligrama. Kuppanna Bhatta sat amidst his worldly possessions, his hand to his forehead, his eyes lowered.

"Aren't cattle part of movable property?" the storekeeper asked.

"Of course," said the ameen.

The town-crier had finished his job and come back. "Go, bring home the cattle grazing on the slopes of the hillock," the ameen told him. Then he went inside and fetched a gunny bag for the assortment of vessels. As he shook the gunny bag, four or five little baby mice, new-born and still pink, fell out of it. They writhed and wriggled in the hot sun. "Eesh," the ameen exclaimed in disgust. "Thath!" said the storekeeper, as a crow hopped in stealthily, and making a sudden lunge, carried off one of the baby mice.

A number of people from Buklapura stood behind the trees around the house. They had ropes and sickles in their hands and pretended to be there in the course of their work. No one dared to step into the courtyard. Not one person made a bid for the goods. "Why should we commit the sin of coveting another's belongings?" some thought. "Cheh! poor man," cried several others, feeling sorry for him. One by one, they moved away from there. Only a few, who could not conquer their curiosity, stayed back to see what would happen.

The agent had the arecanut sacks loaded on to the cart. The ameen made a detailed list of all the articles they had seized. Everything except the brooms, the silver picture, and a couple of broken vessels was placed on to the cart. Without looking at him, the agent admonished Kuppanna Bhatta. "No one who misappropriates that which belongs to Narasimha can survive, let alone prosper. Understand, Bhatta-re? From today, neither the land nor this house is yours. The tenancy has been made over to Appanna Bhatta."

As he heaved himself up into the cart, he fired a last salvo, "Anyway, why should you worry? You have already sent your hoarded wealth with your wife to her parents' place!"

❦

There was an old ajji in Buklapura whose name was Sitakka. No one knew how old she was. She seemed to have been living there from the beginning of time. She addressed everyone in the singular, showing no respect for anyone. Married and widowed when she was still a child, she lived all by herself in a dilapidated little hut. Sitakka had no one to call her own, not even someone to offer a ball of rice at her shraddha when she died. Every day, she begged for a handful of rice to make some kanji for herself, her only meal of the day.

Sitakka had a sharp tongue, and everyone in the agrahara was terrified of her. If the shadow of a lower caste person fell across her path, if children accidentally touched her while they were playing, if she found anyone retreating into their homes at her sight, because she was a widow and hence a bad omen, out poured a stream of imprecations. It was almost as if she could not sleep if she did not spend a couple of hours a day raving and ranting at someone. Perhaps she thought that unless she picked a quarrel and invoked their forefathers for several generations and cursed these evil times, people would take her for granted. Afraid of her abuse, people gave her rice even before she asked for it! After her meal, she spent her time sitting either on the stone steps leading to the river or on the platform outside the temple, twisting cotton into wicks.

At the sound of the town-crier's drum that day, Sitakka's ears perked up. Quickly, she took the mandatory three dips in the river, gulped the kanji and went to find out what had happened. The agrahara seemed to have been emptied of all men. None of the women would tell her anything. Finally she got the information from a farm labourer. Sitakka marched into Kuppanna Bhatta's courtyard. There she saw a couple of misshapen vessels and a few brooms strewn around. Kuppanna Bhatta sat among them, his bald head exposed to the fierce sun.

Sitakka's harsh outburst shattered the oppressive silence. "Which son of a whore has ruined your home? May his house crumble. Let his cattle be seized by tigers. But what is the matter with you? Why are you sitting like this? Have you too begun to believe that a poor man who loses his temper loses his teeth? Where is your arrogance now? Your insolence? You never cared to talk to me, to ask whether I was alive or dead." Kuppanna Bhatta made no reply. Sitakka was puzzled.

"Let the fire swallow your enemy ..." Sitakka began again but stopped when she noticed someone standing under a nearby tree. "Who is that lurking there like a ghost?" she asked, crossing over to him. It was a young man called Narasimha Bhatta from Buklapura. But she did not recognize him. "Who are you? Come here, will you," she said. The man came forward timidly.

Together the two of them held Kuppanna Bhatta by the arms, picked him up and seated him in the shade of the jagali. Quietly, the young man sneaked away.

Cursing Appanna Bhatta, the agent, Kuppanna Bhatta, the other Brahmins of Buklapura and everyone else she could think of, Sitakka picked up the pots and pans scattered around and placed them on the jagali. She saw the lock on the door of the storeroom and heartily cursed the hand that had put it there. "May a snake bite it," she muttered. Then she hastened to her own home, but before that, she stood in front of Appanna Bhatta's house and showered curses on his heartlessness. She got together some avalakki, asked someone for some curds to mix it with, crushed a green chilli into it, added a pinch of salt and took it back to Kuppanna Bhatta. She wrapped it in a banana leaf which she pushed in front of him and ordered, "Eat this. Don't starve yourself like an idiot." Then she went home, took a bath and lay down on the bare floor.

After the sun had set, Appanna Bhatta called one of his labourers and told him, "Go and see what Kuppanna Bhatta is doing – whether he is there or has slunk away to his wife's place. Take care that you're not seen." The servant did as he was told. In the light of the moon, he saw the still, motionless figure on the jagali, and was frightened. He rushed back to report what he had seen.

"See what a schemer he is!" Appanna Bhatta said to his wife. "This is another one of his tricks. Do you know what a drama he put on for the benefit of the agent? I tell you, if he does not creep to his wife's home by the first light of day, my name is not Appanna Bhatta."

The next day dawned. The man who brought in the firewood announced, "He is still sitting on the jagali." Curious to see what was happening, Appanna Bhatta tucked into his waist the key the agent had given him and set off. As he neared Kuppanna Bhatta's house, his heart started thudding. For a while he lingered behind a large tree, pretending to cut down something.

Kuppanna Bhatta was sitting on the jagali, like a stone, his dark body leaning against the wall, his dhotra thrown over his head. Appanna Bhatta's heart missed a beat. As he went nearer, he thought to himself, "If Kuppanna Bhatta picks up a quarrel, I will give him a fitting reply. I will ask him about the wealth that he has already despatched to his in-laws' place." He felt reassured and stepped into the courtyard. A grey dog lay in front of Kuppanna Bhatta, gazing intently at him. A plantain leaf with a small heap of dried-up avalakki on it, lay untouched. Before he realized it, Appanna Bhatta had called out, "Bhatta-re!" There was no reply. With a shaking finger, he jabbed at the figure who continued to sit with his eyes closed.

All the blood had drained out of Kuppanna Bhatta's aged face, leaving it wan and pale. Again, Appanna Bhatta shook him by the shoulder.

Kuppanna Bhatta opened his eyes.

"You need not have been so rough with the agent," Appanna Bhatta started.

There was no reaction, but Kuppanna Bhatta's eyes were open. Appanna Bhatta felt emboldened.

"What do you lack, Bhatta-re? You have carried your hatred of me this long. But I don't hold it against you. After all, you are older than me. As an elder, you should wish me well. That's what I want. You should not leave with hard feelings against me. So I have come to speak to you. I shall send you to your brother-in-law's house in my own cart. Come and eat a meal in my house before you go. Let us forget this enmity of thirty years."

Appanna Bhatta had not meant to go so far. One word had led to another without his realizing it. Kuppanna Bhatta's continued silence had made him raise his own voice. But it appeared as though his words did not penetrate the other man's eardrums. Not a muscle on Kuppanna Bhatta's face moved. His stillness hit Appanna Bhatta with the force of a blow. And Appanna Bhatta was speechless. After a while, he recovered. As he paced up and down the courtyard, he continued, more softly this time, "I have not done anything to ruin you, Bhatta-re. For thirty years I have endured your resentment. But did I ever try to compete with you? It is true that I informed the agent that Narasimha's share of the produce was being diverted to Gopala Kamti's account. If I am not telling the truth, let my tongue split into two. Call the elders of Buklapura and let them adjudicate. If they find that I am in the wrong, I shall fall at your feet."

Appanna Bhatta's voice became shrill. "Last year you took away all those growers who used to supply arecanut to me. When you had money to trade, was it right to default on your payments of rent? Wouldn't anyone get angry at that? Aren't there some rules in such matters? Like you, I am a man with a family. Like you, I have a daughter to marry off too. I also have my troubles. For the past year, I have been suffering from some ailment of the stomach. I am in constant pain. Last month, my buffalo, which used to give a bucketful of milk, suddenly died. It is all our fate, Bhatta-re. Come on. Get up and come with me. Have a meal at my place. I will get the bullock-cart ready and you can start for your brother-in-law's place in the cool hours of the evening."

The grey mongrel looked at one face, then at the other, and then at the avalakki on the plantain leaf. Kuppanna Bhatta's eyes stared vacantly past Appanna Bhatta and into the forest beyond. Appanna Bhatta felt his throat go dry in the oppressive silence. He kept repeating, "Bhatta-re, Bhatta-re ..." as if he were reciting the names of his ancestors during a shraddha. The dog rose, stretched its limbs, and lay down again. Mango-gnats hovered around. The sunlight blazed.

Kuppanna Bhatta sat on his haunches, resting his head on his palm and his elbow on his knees, a towel over his head. Appanna Bhatta looked at him again, as if seeing him for the first time. There was a churning feeling in his stomach.The avalakki on the banana leaf was dry, though it had once been soaked in curds. Flies sat on it. And flies sat on Kuppanna Bhatta's nose. Once every few seconds, he blinked.

"Bhatta-re, I don't want your property. Stay on in your house. I will let you cultivate this land as long as you live. Just pay me the rent every year. I am not a butcher. Like you I came from the coast with an empty copper vessel in my hand. All I want is that I should not drop dead in a jungle path as my father did. There was no one even to pour a few drops of water down his throat as he was dying. When I found him, lying there in the sun, the crows were pecking at him. I pray that kind of death does not come to me, that's all, Bhatta-re. Here, take your keys. Keep them," Appanna Bhatta cried. Overcome with emotion, he blew his nose.

The man who sat there on his haunches, as if waiting for his last breath, showed no reaction. This still, shrouded figure seemed to burn into Appanna Bhatta's mind and his tongue, never lacking in fluency, grew silent too. Appanna Bhatta put his towel over his head and he too squatted on the jagali, opposite the silent one.

THE DYNAMICS OF TEXTUALITY

An Essay

When a writer creates a text, the process of creation – and this happens often in the case of the modern Indian writer – is not a celebratory retelling of memories, stored in oral traditions but a critical reinterpretation and recreation of memories. It is a constant struggle against vismruti – loss of memory. Thus there is a paradox in this dynamics: unless you forget, there is no movement in time, no renewal, and therefore no impetus to new creation. Also, unless you recover your past, the usable past, under the stress of the present, there is no creation either. Continuity is the very essence of the human condition in these ever-changing times –

continuity in our own biological life span, as well as with our purva suris, our sage ancestors.

Even now, in remote villages, people sitting around a blacksmith's forge, or sitting under a tree where the village barber plies his trade, tell each other stories. There is an effortless and delightful sharing in this exercise. The listeners punctuate their hearing with Hu hu – Yes, yes – thus egging on the narrator to share with them what is already known, but still to be renewed as experience. The audience participating in such an experience is a living community. Its presence in the narrative experience is immediate.

We, the contemporary Indian writers, are different from them, although our creativity originates from them. We are surrounded by them and, in fact, derive the shabda shakti from them. When a writer like me writes a story, my ideal listener is myself. The story, incidentally, is also being read by my reader. Not aloud in a family gathering, but to himself, silently, when he is alone. His mind may wander away, and he can close the book and look away. He is free. Utter freedom is the very condition of the act of reading. I offer my narration to such a solitary and voluntary attention of the free reader. Hence a modern text assumes that in order to be authentic, unpleasant truths ought to be shared with the reader, who is, for a while at least, prepared to suspend his membership of his community.

Reading, and writing, thus, is an asocial act – an act outside of our obligations and privileges within the shared assumptions of our communities. Again, there is a paradox here. It is our deepest desire to belong authentically to our community, which prompts us both to read and write, this way – for we want to renew ourselves in the naked truth of our experience and shed all falseness and dishonest acquiescence to the ideological imperatives of our communities. Such truths may be implicitly acknowledged in communal storytelling under the tree, or in the artisans's workshop, but it is all the metaphors and myths which make a subliminal

---

This essay was first published in *Indian Horizons*, 1992.

appeal. I think that communication in utter solitude has become the feature of at least some of our modern written narratives. For, there is more correspondence to the real in such a textual narrative, and in such "truthful" telling, and causing embarrassment is a way of keeping awake our consciences. What I mean is this: we often write because we have a problem with our communities which we want to sort out in solitude. This is done, as ruthlessly as possible, so that we can belong again to our common humanity, authentically, being cleansed in the process of the dynamics of the text revealed in silent communication.

❦

Whereas the need to please, entertain, and enhance attention thereby is the motivation in oral story telling, in genuine written texts, the motivating force may be to encounter embarrassment and communicate it to the reader – which is spiritually healing. Without such reflection or meditation, there is no real participation in one's own community. Tolstoy's fascination and repulsion of the erotic element in life, the loss of faith and suffering of Dostoevsky's characters, and Tagore's darshan of the ultimate truth through *Gora*, are instances of the peculiar nature of our great modern texts. These are distinguished from oral narratives – not necessarily in their content – for oral narratives also may contain such encounters with the unpleasant – but in the effect of sudden recognition they produce on their silent solitary readers. The presence of the community has a soothing effect on the listener in oral renderings. Ideally speaking, this should be absent in communication of a certain kind of modern text. Such an absence of community is essential for the communicated experience of the text.

These are very general observations and it would not be correct unless I relate them to my own experience of writing. I offer myself as a case, not because I think that I am of much significance, nor that I may be typical. I do so only to provoke a dialogue among other writers to examine the subtle forces at work in their own narratives. Please watch, I may even disagree with the claim I make of texts, when I begin later on to think of the response of the readers. (Whatever be my own intentions in producing the written artefact).

It was nearly a little more than twenty-five years ago that I wrote *Samskara*. The process of writing was an intense experience. I was in England as a student, and fatigued with speaking the English language most of the time . I needed to recover my mother-tongue, living in the midst of English, my father-tongue, to use an expression of Ramanujan.

It all started when I went to see a Bergman film – *Seventh Seal* – with my teacher, the famous novelist and critic, Malcolm Bradbury. The film had no sub-titles. My incomplete comprehension of it started a vague stirring in me. I remember having told Dr Bradbury that a European has no living memory of the middle ages and hence constructs it through knowledge acquired from books.. But for an Indian like me, centuries coexist as a living memory transmitted through oral traditions. This set me off to rewrite a story which I had originally written for a journal. Called *Tarangini*, this manuscript-magazine was edited by a group of High School students, and circulated among our elders in the agrahara. It contained articles in three languages – Sanskrit, English and Kannada.

What had prompted me to write this story as a boy was a series of incidents that had disturbed me during those days when I walked to the school in the taluka headquarters from my village every day. There had been a plague in Tirthahalli, the taluka headquarters, and a doctor came to inoculate us in the village. Being a brahmin, he did not go to the colony of the untouchables. A little later, the harijans in the colony began to die of plague. The elders in the agrahara interpreted this as a punishment from heaven for the harijans, who inspired by Gandhiji's teachings, had dared to enter some temples far away in the north.

At school, I had been exposed to new ideas, and to Mahatma

Gandhi's writings which my father used to read aloud to his friends. So I was a little sceptical about the rumours floating around in the village. Also, I knew a secret which I could not share with anyone else. A young man from the agrahara who had joined the Army had come back home. He had been to distant places and would talk to us about them. We looked at him with awe and wonder and believed him to be a truly modern man. I knew that he was having a secret affair with one of the pretty harijan girls.

When entire families began to die, the harijans, who had no other possessions, set fire to their thatch-and-mud huts. Most of them died like this, passively accepting it as their fate. But the girl ran away from our village and disappeared mysteriously. I then wrote a metaphorical story based on those incidents. Metaphorical, because I dared not speak the truth to my elders. The theme of the story was this – since she had been touched, a new awareness was aroused in her. Thus *touch* became an important motif and theme for me from my thirteenth year.

I began to rewrite this story in England and it became *Samskara*. I can never forget the experience of writing this in England as I was surrounded by a reality utterly different from what I had experienced as a village boy. I began to see things in my own distant past very clearly. I think the distance in time and space helped me to recover smells and sounds and gestures which were buried within me.

I sent the manuscript to the Kannada poet, Gopalakrishna Adiga who wrote back to say that he liked the story but it seemed incomplete. I sat down again and wondered how I should continue the story. I felt as if I heard footsteps following my hero who was wandering away. I wondered who was following my hero. Thus came to my novel a character who made the act of writing very lively for me. This was the half-caste Putta – the Other in my novel, who complicated and enriched my theme.

Those of you who have read my novel know that he talks incessantly and that he is a bit of a village buffoon and a typical oral story teller. When I created him, I remembered the gypsy in *Seventh*

Seal. Was I also retelling for myself another great Kannada story by Shivram Karanth that I had read in High School? *Back to the Soil* is the name of this novel in translation. One of the characters in this novel was a wasteful man who, tempted by the attractions of urban life, rebelled against the sacred norms of domestic life. The name of this character and the name of the rebel in my novel are similar. After many years, it has struck me that I was trying to understand, metaphorically and symbolically, something that was described realistically by Karanth. Thus Bergman, Karanth and Marxism on which I was working at that time, Adiga's influence, the influence of existentialist novels that I was reading, and the memories of my boyhood days entered into my narrative in a magical manner. I had a feeling that I was exceeding myself as I wrote this novel.

Now I want to ask some questions about myself. As a child, I had grown up in an oral tradition. All my knowledge of epics and of the shastras had been gathered not by reading, but through Yakshagana and harikatha and through listening to debates during ritual meals in a monastery. If I was not deeply affected by these, I could not have written this novel. At the same time, if I was merely like my other relatives, I would have been trained in a pathasala and I would have given my life to learning by heart the *Rigveda*. Had I submitted myself to such a discipline and lived an orthodox life, I wonder whether I would have had the need to write the novel I wrote.

Not only that, I must ask another question. I was born in an orthodox family where my father had moved away from the vaidic ways which my grandfather followed, and became a loukik. He had been exposed to the influence of Gandhi. Therefore, my self-taught father had sent me for English studies. As a consequence, I had found myself inevitably drawn into the process of modernization. I still remember how my father insisted on my learning, by heart, Edmund Burke's famous impeachment speech of Warren Hastings as seriously as he had wanted me to memorize the *Purusha Sukta*.

Thus my father had launched me on a path where it was

inevitable for me to question and doubt the world in which I lived. I even got married outside my own religion and community, thereby breaking away from my ritualistic traditional life. This was not an easy thing to do. It had produced a terror in my heart at the time of breaking away. Was I recapturing this fear when I wrote my novel? In other words, if I had entirely belonged to my oral traditions, I would perhaps not have written this novel. At the same time, if my childhood was different and purely urban and hence not exposed to oral traditions, I wouldn't have written this novel either.

❦

I had believed, after finishing my novel, that I have written a self-contained modern novel almost like a hall of mirrors, to use Dr Kelkar's image. But the way my readers responded to it, my novel turned into a room with a view – again to use another image of Kelkar. In my agrahara, people who had loved me once, now censured me for putting some of them in my novel. Thus they responded to the novel literally. And a little distance from my village, at the district level, people thought that I was attacking a certain sect of the brahmins – the Madhwa brahmins. As the novel further moved in space, it was seen more abstractly as anti-brahmin in the state of Karnataka. V S. Naipaul, who was even further away, read it as a critique of Hinduism. Further away still, when Erik Erikson saw the film and read the novel, he saw it as a depiction of the crisis of middle age. What I want to ask here is this: Which is my novel? Whose response is truer from the point of view of the printed text – my own people in the agrahara who read it literally, or the people from other cultures who read it symbolically?

My whole submission at this seminar is intended to raise a single question as sharply as possible. There is a break with the oral traditions when a writer writes a book. It has a curious kind of existence if it is born in a context where oral traditions are still very alive, as they are in our country. The text is also largely read by a middle-class audience who are in the process of distancing themselves from their own traditions, because of the process of modernization. Hence the text may become a self-conscious attempt at recovering memory and interpreting it critically. In other words, the text uses memory not to celebrate existence, but to question one's own existence. May I then say that a text has a profoundly critical function which oral traditions need not have?

The Crafting Years

1932	Born on December 21 in Melige, a village in Karnataka.
1955	*Endendu Mugiyada Kathe*, his first collection of short stories, is published.
1956	He finishes his MA and is awarded a Gold Medal by the University of Mysore. He is appointed Lecturer in English at the same university.
1963	His first book of poems, *Bavali*, is published. He receives the Commonwealth Fellowship and leaves for the UK.
1965	*Samskara*, his first novel, appears in print.
1966	He receives a doctorate from the University of Birmingham, UK.
1967	He joins the Regional College of Education in Mysore as a Reader in English.
1970	The Best Story Award is conferred on him for the film *Samskara*.
1971	His first play, *Avahane*, is published.
1972	He receives the Homi Bhabha Fellowship for Creative Writing.
1975	He is a Visiting Writer and Professor at the University of Iowa.
1978	The Best Story Award is again presented to him. This time it is for the film *Ghatashraddha*. He is made a member of the General Council of the Sahitya Akademi. He is a Visiting Professor in English at Tufts University.
1980	He is appointed a member of the Academic Council of Mysore University and the General Secretary of the People's Union of Civil Liberties (Karnataka).
1981	He takes on the editorship of the journal *Rujuvathu*.
1982	He is a Visiting Professor at the Shivaji University in Kolhapur
1983	The Karnataka Sahitya Akademi Award for Fiction is conferred on him.

1984 He receives the Karnataka Government Award for Literary Distinction and the Karnataka Sahitya Akademi Award for Literary Achievement.

1985 He is the Ida Beam Visiting Professor at the University of Iowa.

1986 He is a Fulbright Scholar-in-Residence at the University of Iowa.

1987 He is appointed Vice-Chancellor of the Mahatma Gandhi University in Kottayam.

1988 He receives the Samaj Bhushan from the the Swamiji of the Admar Matha. He visits Denmark on a lecture tour.

1989 The movie *Bara* earns him his third Best Story Award. A lecture tour takes him to North Korea and China.

1990 The Harmony Award is presented to him.

1992 He is the Chairman of the National Book Trust. He visits Germany to teach at the University of Tubingen.

1993 Appointed President of the Sahitya Akademi, he is also a Visiting Professor at the Jawaharlal Nehru University in Delhi.

1994 He receives the Masti Award in Literature.

1995 The Rabindra Bharati University in Calcutta confers an honorary doctorate on him and he is a Writer-in-Residence at the University of Texas at Austin. He also receives the Katha Award for Creative Fiction for his most recent story, "Akkayya."

1995 U R Anantha Murthy is honoured with the Jnanpith Award for his outstanding contribution to literature.

BHUPEN KHAKHAR

"I don't want to go to art as if I were going to pray. Seriousness is only a small part of ourselves. Much about us is frivolous."

– Bhupen Khakhar

The vulgar interests him. He thinks good taste can be very killing. The values and the taste of the Indian lower middle classes, into which he was born, are both celebrated and satirized in his work. Garish colours, mock chandeliers, hideous advertisements and caricatured figures feature in his paintings. His stories talk about the hypocrisy and idiosyncrasies of the middle class, their double standards, the lack of an organic relationship between themselves and their homes. From this scathingly satiric vision, what emerges is a gently comic view of the world, a tongue-in-cheek appraisal of issues that seem to shake the existence of the lesser mortals.

Bhupen Khakhar just refuses to take himself seriously. Chesterton once remarked, "Angels can fly because they take themselves lightly," and Bhupen Khakhar certainly looks like an innocent little cherub on the brink of his maiden flight. Exactly as he must have looked years ago, in 1965, when he had the critics spluttering in rage at the Jehangir Art Gallery in Bombay. This accountant-turned-painter from Bombay had actually torn up harmless, ambivalent oleographs from gaudy, popular calendars, pasted them on to canvas, brushed them up with some gestural paintwork, added graffiti, and inscribed the legend: It is prohibited to urinate here.

Thirty years on, Bhupen Khakhar remains as irrepressible as ever. Whether it is an innocent question eliciting his opinion on the Gujarat State Lalit Kala Akademi, to which he has only the cryptic counter-question, "You want us to burn it?" Or it is the more "serious" issue of the East's cultural identity vis-a-vis the West's, to which he responds indignantly, "With French art, the question of how much America has influenced it never arises. Or whether pop art has influenced English art ... Why can't an Indian artist use a Western influence without being questioned about it?"

The son of a cloth merchant and a schoolteacher, Bhupen Khakhar was born in Bombay on March 10, 1934. "I was brought up in a lower middle-class family, as were most of my friends. We all lived in chawls and one-room apartments – that image is still with me when I write." After graduating in Economics and Commerce from Wilson College, he joined a firm of chartered accountants. But in 1961, he announced his intention to be a painter and, in the face of great familial opposition, he gave up his job and left Bombay for Baroda to enrol in a master's course in Criticism at the Faculty of Fine Arts. "Nobody in the family was talking to me. CA, bungalow, car, flourishing practice, a queue of girls waiting to be matched ... all their dreams were shattered," he recalls.

Working part-time as an accountant, he started painting in earnest.

"I don't want ..." is a quote from Bhupen Khakhar in an interview with Eunice de Souza in *The Times Weekly*, January 17, 1971.

This was also when his stories began to appear in Gujarati journals. Today, he still lives in Baroda, and his paintings sell for a fortune each.

Always critical about the eclectic West-oriented Indian artist, Khakhar cannot understand the artist's need to close himself up in stuffy attics in order to paint. His ideal workplace is the window facing the street from where he can wave to his shopkeeper friends, and not the artist's attic. Also, unlike the typical picture of the bohemian artist working away into the wee hours of the morning, Khakhar follows a strict routine. A chartered accountant till 2 pm every day, he does not feel that he has fulfilled his role as a responsible social citizen until he has contributed that bit of service to the community. Friends come and go frequently at his specially-designed house-cum-studio in Baroda and these social encounters are reflected in his artistic as well as literary outputs.

Khakhar's abiding preoccupation has been human relationships. He speaks "of human bondage" in this life. To live is to link, and thus form the chain that binds, that hurts, that joins in companionship, conspiracy or common activity. Everywhere, all the time, human beings forge or break ties with their kinspeople. Which is why the dilemma of being different from the rest is so acute a predicament in the Indian social setup. The final challenge to human bondages came when he announced his homosexuality on canvas. "I was a coward," he admitted(in a recent interview in the magazine *Outlook).* "I told lies. I did not have the courage to say I was going to meet my boyfriend. Only at the age of sixty, after much travel and exposure to these things abroad, I have summoned courage to speak about my preferences."

Bhupen Khakhar's works have always borne the stamp of his unique personality. "Influences" is a four-letter word for this iconoclast who came from the chawls of Bombay to storm the bastions of the oh-so-propah Indian art. And went on to win the Padma Shri. In his own eyes, though, he does not think of himself as a particularly rebellious artist. "There is no element of revolt in anything I paint, but a total acceptance of a situation. I don't revolt against vulgarity, I enjoy it." His world is the very real one peopled by men and women whose only topic of conversation may be the dinner menu of the house next door and the rumour-mongering rampant in any middle-class locality. "People who are not educated can sometimes write very well. Their own experience is distilled in their writing," he says, and his writing sure proves him right!

Now, as always, Bhupen Khakhar continues to draw from life for his subjects, but in a manner not normally understood to be "artistic." Khakhar's world admits of a dominant sense of theatre, some bawdiness and, above all, an innate wisdom. Looking back, he says, "We often make social adjustments in order to please people. We forget our duty to ourselves. What we should do in life and art is to do exactly what we like. The difficulty, maybe, is to find out what one likes." So today, at the age of sixty-one, he lives in Baroda and paints and writes. And now, his latest venture brings both his vocations together – his story "Phoren Soap" is about to be published in limited editions with prints of woodcuts done by him, specially for it.

Bhupen Khakhar does not offer the comfort of accepted, acceptable norms, nor does he spout bitter, heavy philosophy. Dramatizing the incidental and the ordinary by straightforward representation is the characteristic quality of his work. For him, art is not bound by the strictures of etiquette or good taste. Instead, his creativity bursts forth like a sudden monsoon shower, like an airy balloon ride, like the gurgling laughter of an angel or the antics of a Shakespearean Puck.

BHUPEN KHAKHAR

in conversation with
G N Devy & U Nanavati

Bhupen Khakhar lives in Baroda in a house built in the surrealistic style – a house with intriguing spaces that seem to serve no purpose. The furniture belongs to what can only be termed the "Bhupen Khakhar" period. In fact, everything in the house bears the distinctive mark of his personality, his sense of humour, and his way of organizing symbols. We met him on a pleasant November morning and spoke to him about his writing and his paintings.

GD: *Bhupen, when did you realize that reality can be represented through two distinct mediums – one of colour and the other of words?*

And what, to you, is the difference between these two mediums?

BK: I'll have to go back many, many years to answer that. This was when I was studying at Wilson College. I used to write as well as paint. My first story was published in *The Wilsonian*, our college magazine. Those days, I used to draw a little too, though I had not had any formal training. For a long while, I could not make up my mind whether I should choose painting or writing as a career.

I have always found writing to be a very confessional mode of expression. Painting, at that time, seemed to be much more objective. So I chose to concentrate on painting. Then in the 70s I realized that some things could be articulated only through words. And I started writing short stories again. A few poems too, but I soon realized that poetry was not my cup of tea.

***GD:** Your readership is necessarily limited because you write only in Gujarati. Did that at all affect your decision to pay greater attention to painting?*

BK: Very few people have any respect for my writing. I feel I am not acceptable as a writer, in a way. The Gujarati Lalit Kala Akademi recently published a directory of writers. There are about eight hundred names in it but mine is not one of those. People have accepted me as a painter and so there is a greater demand for my paintings. Or rather, I get more opportunities in that area.

IN THE 70S I REALIZED THAT SOME THINGS COULD BE ARTICULATED ONLY THROUGH WORDS. AND I STARTED WRITING SHORT STORIES AGAIN.

***GD:** You began as a very non-conventional painter and showed scant regard for established styles. So wasn't it difficult being accepted even as a painter?*

BK: It was! Years ago, when I had exhibited some of my works in college, they were torn off. Later at the Jehangir Art Gallery, the Secretary asked me to remove two or three paintings. Even as late as 1986, the Gallery asked me not to exhibit some representations of sexuality that I had done. I had to put my foot down and say, "If you don't display these paintings, then I won't have my show at all." They agreed, but the moment I left, they removed one painting from the display. This kind of thing kept happening till '86. Not any more.

GD: *So what happened in 1986? Was it a turning point of sorts?*

BK: I can't recall if it was '86 or '84. But I know that since the 80s, I have become bolder in terms of the things I represent.

GD: *There is at once a spiritual element as well as a measure of popular culture in your work. Is this a reflection of your personality?*

BK: I don't know about the spiritual bit, but I can say that I have always been drawn to things which are on the periphery of art, which are not acceptable as art – popular music, popular writing. Besides these, I am interested in hybrid culture too. I have noticed that when the East and the West meet the result is quite strange.

GD: *Bombay is full of people and really the site of popular culture. Whereas Baroda still has the ambience of a princely-feudalistic social structure. Why did you move from Bombay to Baroda?*

BK: It's not as if I don't like Bombay. I used to work as a chartered accountant and, if I'd stayed on, I think my family would not have allowed me to paint. Besides I did not have enough space there. I was brought up in a lower middle-class family, as were most of my friends. We all lived in chawls and in one-room apartments – that image is still with me when I write. While, Baroda had this Faculty of Fine Arts, and so many of my artist friends lived here. Hence the move.

GD: *Who are your favourite painters?*

BK: Indian or Western?

GD: *Whichever – those who matter, whose work you enjoy, who might have inspired you.*

BK: Influences keep changing. I used to like Henri Rousseau's paintings. Then there was a period when I liked Hockney's paintings – that was in the 70s. Then I liked Matisse. Then Breughel.

GD: *What do you think of the ethnic revival in painting? There has been quite a tradition, beginning with Ravi Varma. You too have painted temples and saints and festivals. But what is your attitude to Indian deities? You have depicted them as fairly absurd figures in your play* Mojila Manilal.

BK: I am somewhat of an iconoclast. In 1965, I had taken oleographs of divinities from popular calendars, stuck them on to canvas, and painted over them. That upset people, I think. To them, gods are sacrosanct. My play refutes that. I have shown that it rains in the fields of both Badman as well as Goodman – the gods don't make any distinction there. Good deeds don't get you a place in heaven. The gods decide that – with a roll of the dice.

GD: *Is this why Salman Rushdie admires your work so much and wanted you to paint his portrait?*

BK: I think there is – there may be – something that we have in common. I have known him for many years – since '79. He had come to my exhibition in London. He liked my work but did not have money to buy any of it. He came again. Since he had sold two stories to the *New Yorker* by then, he bought one of my paintings.

As for the portrait, I don't think Rushdie had requested it. It was the BBC, in consultation with him and the gallery. We were meeting after a long time. While he sat for me – for almost five hours daily – he would talk about *The Moor's Last Sigh*.

I HAVE NOTICED THAT WHEN THE EAST AND THE WEST MEET THE RESULT IS QUITE STRANGE.

***GD:** Apart from Rushdie, who are the writers you enjoy reading?*

BK: There are quite a few. *(laughs)*

***GD:** In Gujarati?*

BK: In Gujarati? Few, very few.

***GD:** You told me once that you find it difficult to appreciate contemporary writing in Gujarati since it has moved very far from the language of the people.*

BK: I find the problem is that – in our work – we consider everything to be sacred. That's not true of the way we live though. We are very frivolous, we joke about all kinds of things, including life. But when we come to painting or writing, or even discussion, we suddenly turn very serious – as if this is something holy, as if it's puja. That's the attitude I dislike. Which is why I find popular culture, even popular detective novels, much more entertaining. They don't want to impress you, they don't seem to be saying, Look how serious I am!

We don't even have a good writer of detective fiction in Gujarati. In the West, there are so many people who are serious writers but they can also entertain you, like Simenon, Le Carre. We totally lack that. Our writing is too self-oriented, too autobiographical.

***GD:** What strikes one immediately about your work is the inherent humour and the way you make symbols out of ordinary objects. Is it because you feel that the humorous mode is more effective than the tragic?*

BK: I think so. I have always felt that we get too much of the tragic stuff – even on TV. In the serial on the *Mahabharat*, one scene in every episode had to show women crying. I found that very irritating. It is very easy, I feel – and I may be wrong – to write in the sentimental mode. So I don't. Why shouldn't I use humour instead? And it is more a part of me.

***GD:** Do you read short stories by other writers?*

BK: Yes, I do. I read quite a bit now, especially writers like Milan Kundera. Also a lot of detective fiction.

GD: *But what you have written as stories don't conform to any established models of story writing. Suresh Joshi, who made a major impact on the Gujarati short story, was a close friend of yours. But in your fiction, I don't detect any influence at all of his ideas or his work.*

BK: I don't think he liked my stories. He considered them, I think, too rough, too vulgar. They don't have his kind of delicacy or even an elegant use of language. His language is very delicate. He goes to Sanskrit literature, then to Bangla literature and makes it all very poetic. My stories don't have that quality. But later on, at least at the end, Suresh Joshi did like my paintings.

GD: *Your stories, translated into English in the* Bombay Literary Review *and* Katha Prize Stories, *for instance, have been received well. In fact, Dilip Chitre, who has read your work only in translation, once said that you represent the best in Gujarati literature. Do you think that your stories read better in translation?*

BK: No, I think they read well in Gujarati. Or perhaps even in Marathi, since there is so much in common between the two languages. But a lot is lost in English.

GOOD DEEDS DON'T GET YOU A PLACE IN HEAVEN. THE GODS DECIDE THAT – WITH A ROLL OF THE DICE.

GD: *Do you think that sex occupies too large a space in your work – writing and painting?*

BK: It does.

GD: *Would you like to defend that?*

BK: No, I don't see the need to. It is the most natural thing in life.

GD: *Bhupen, in* Mojila Manilal, *you have one man falling in love with two women, both married. Was this character based on someone you know?*

Or was it a deliberate attempt to attack prudery in Gujarati society?

BK: I did have someone in mind. I knew him in Bombay. He had a shop next to my brother's. I ran into him at the Ahmedabad Station once and he insisted that I should accompany him. He took me to a chawl where two women were making pickles. He started flirting with both of them and they too responded. I found that strange. Not only strange, but also entertaining since they were in their forties, he in his early sixties. This was the starting point for the play – two women sharing a man and not being jealous of each other. Anyway, this is nothing compared to what happens in chawls. So much for our moral prudery!

GD: *What else do you do besides paint/write? I know you travel quite a bit – not only abroad but also in India. What intrigues me, is where do you get so much energy and enthusiasm – you almost seem addicted to travelling.*

BK: When I travel, I leave behind in Baroda, my usual concerns, so if I want to write, I do just that. Or if I am painting, then I find I am full of ideas.

Besides, for all art you need new horizons, new places. Wherever I travel, I always carry my sketch book with me. So I draw – sometimes I sketch – even in crowded trains. It is for these travel notes or sketches that I keep going to Bundi, Kota, Delhi, Ahmedabad. If I am always in Baroda, my view will be a limited one. I can do water colours and other things like that when I am out travelling. But for oil painting I've got to be in Baroda.

GD: *In your work and otherwise, do you deliberately try to avoid making political statements?*

BK: I'm interested in what Gandhiji had to say, though I may not follow all his rules. He is one person who really interests me. But I don't care much about other political ideologies. What upsets me is the Hindu-Muslim tension. I've done a few small water colour paintings about that. But ...

GD: *I remember, once when we went to Kanpur together, you were sketching as we floated on the Ganga in a ferry boat. Did that experience, those temples and ghats, evoke a feeling of reverence in you? I am curious to know how all that affected you.*

BK: No, it wasn't reverence that I had felt then. It was very exciting, visually.

GD: *Do you take an interest in the other arts, such as music, dance?*

BK: *(laughs)* I like popular Hindi film music, and some classical Indian music. I've no ear for Western music and I am not interested in dance.

GD: *Bhupen, are you aware that you are a very singular person, both as a writer and as a painter?*

BK: Whenever I see the works of other artists, I feel very inferior. I feel, Why the hell am I painting? Why am I writing when so many extraordinary writers have written so much and so well?

GD: *Your recent story, which was called "Phoren Soap" even in Gujarati, has created quite a stir. I have heard friends talk of it in other cities too, though it is not really widely circulated in published form. I understand that you have done some visuals for that story too. Can you tell us a little about it?*

BK: The story is based on the belief, particularly of the middle-class person, that everything which is foreign is good. When people go to the custom free goods shop, they buy things, a lot of things. I think this was the starting point. One sentence came to my mind, "Jeevan Lal ne lagyo ke saali phoren soap ne to majaich kain aur che!" (Jeevan Lal

I THINK MY WHOLE VISION AND VOCABULARY IS INTRINSICALLY INDIAN.

felt that the pleasure one gets out of a foreign soap, is something altogether different.) Once I had put that down on paper, the entire story flowed out. There were certain visual things which I felt would add to the story. I did etchings for it even while I was writing it. It was an exciting process. Now that story has been completed, I'm getting it translated into English and am planning to print it in limited editions. The story is not a long one. It is about fourteen to fifteen pages long. The etchings have to be done by hand, so it will take quite a long time. And then the whole book has to be designed too.

GD: *Your paintings are widely appreciated all over the world. Weren't you ever tempted to settle abroad – you'd also get better quality paper and paints there? What keeps you rooted to India?*

BK: I think my whole vision and vocabulary is intrinsically Indian. I can stay elsewhere for a month or two, but I begin to feel restless after that.

GD: *You said that you have great respect for Gandhiji. But your views on sex are quite different from his.*

BK: As I said I respect him though I don't practise everything he preached.

GD: *Naipaul has said that the ego field of an Indian is an ill-formed ego field – a person remains too involved in himself. But it is nice to have someone like you around and I hope that one day you will write a good detective novel for us.*

BK: I have already written it but I've got to revise it. About 150 pages long, it's a short novel. But I'm too lazy to revise it really. You mentioned Naipaul ... a painter friend of mine, Timothy Hyman, told me once – he also writes on art – that most Indian artists are so preoccupied with themselves that they want to talk only about themselves, and about their work. They are not interested in other people. Say, if someone comes to my place, I can show him my work, but I should also be interested in him – this feeling is what Indian artists and writers lack.

GD: *We are bound by our culture.* (BK laughs) *Now the last question. It is in the nature of a reminiscence. I remember, in the last week of October '92, the Katha people had taken us to the Rashtrapati Bhavan for the Awards Ceremony. That was the only time I went to the Rashtrapati Bhavan – perhaps you have been there several times before.*

BK: No, not several. Two-three times, that's all. *(laughs)*

GD: *So how do you relate to that experience?*

BK: This is quite a question. Once I had gone when I was awarded the Padma Shri. Then another time I had gone to meet a friend who was working at the Rashtrapati Bhavan – Jogen Chaudhuri. This was quite an experience. What I liked about President Shankar Dayal Sharma was that he spoke about other languages. And today what has happened is that Hindi, whether you are a good writer or not, the predominance of Hindi is so great that we hardly know what is being written in other languages

GD: *Thank you for giving us so much time. And we wish you all the best – a sentiment I know you won't appreciate.*

BK: *(Laughs)* Thank you.

VADKI

translated by
Naushil Mehta

Jamna lay flat on the bed, staring vacantly at the ceiling. She was unhappy. She had diligently finished with her chores – she did the sweeping, the laundering and the washing of utensils herself, since Jamnadas and she were the only members of the household.

Jamna and Jamnadas had entered into an agreement on their wedding night. The contractual document was on stamp paper, duly signed by both parties. Its contents covered every possible eventuality of their married life. Each of them preserved a copy of this document in a safe place.

So when late at night, in the throes of arousal, Jamna begged for a child, it was a copy of this document that Jamnadas brought out and read aloud from.

> **Section 9, Sub-Section (a)**
> With this, the signatories of the contract, Jamnadas Bapalal and Jamna Jamnadas agree to abide by the decision that: Should any aspect of our personal relationship, be it embraces, kisses, foreplay, play, afterplay or joint read-aloud sessions of the erotic classics, result in the desire for a child, we shall consciously suppress all such activity/activities, bathe ceremoniously in cold water, uproot this desire, and banish it.

The reading and implementation of this Sub-Section invariably proved to be an effective deterrent for desire of all kinds – including that for a child – and brought Jamna's feet down to earth, even metaphorically.

After much pondering and planning, Wednesdays and Saturdays were finalized for lovemaking. Jamna had expressed a desire to celebrate three days of intimacy in the place of just two before signing on the dotted line. The dialogue:

Jamna: If you don't mind, could we amend Section 10, Sub-Section (b)?

Jamnadas: What amendment do you want to propose?

Jamna: You have indicated Wednesday and Saturday for pleasures of the flesh. I feel that this programme should be scheduled thrice a week, say, every Thursday, Saturday and Sunday. That way the body would have more opportunities per week to partake in the play of Goddess Rati. I vote for Thursdays, Saturdays and Sundays.

Jamnadas: Taking our youth into account, I am tempted to accept the proposed amendment. But consider this: My father Bapalal had to summon a carpenter the day he turned fifty. He had a double-bed sawn into two right in front of our entire family.

Jamna: Why?

Till date Bhupen Khakhar has not compiled his short stories in a volume. They have been published in various literary periodicals in Gujarati. This translation was first published in *The Bombay Literary Review*, 1990

Jamnadas: Because the attraction he had once felt for Ba's body had waned. Energies had dwindled. From that day on, Bapuji's cot lay next to the window in the drawing room and Ba's bed was made in the inner room.
Jamna: So what do you propose?
Jamnadas: If it is wished that the capacity for pleasure should last, the principle of two days a week must be observed. And I would still say Wednesdays and Saturdays.
Jamna: Why those days specifically?
Jamnadas: Sunday being a holiday, we can sleep late on account of activities of mutual recreation. Mondays and Tuesdays come too soon after that.
Jamna: Why not Thursdays?
Jamnadas: Thursdays are for fasting. Weakened bodies generate Kama with difficulty.
So Section 10 (a) was constituted thus:

> **Section 10, Sub-Section (a)**
> We, the husband-and-wife signatories of this document, hereby do declare that we will celebrate physical intimacies every Wednesday and Saturday till the time Jamnadas Bapalal turns fifty. If and when such an event comes to pass, Jamnadas has the option of calling a carpenter to saw the double-bed into two.

The tragic look on Jamna's face at this time had inspired Jamnadas to compose a new clause:

> **Section 10, Sub-Section (b)**
> In addition to the provisions made in Section 10 (a), we, the signatories of this document, agree to consider the option of celebrating Full Moon, No Moon, Moon-in-the-Sixth-Phase (ascendant and descendant), and Birthday Nights by mutual consent.

After the inclusion of this Sub-Section, Jamna had happily agreed to Wednesdays and Saturdays.

Today their marital life is a happy one because they have strictly adhered to the Sections and Sub-Sections of this document. Jamnadas is fifty-two and yet no carpenter has as much as touched their double-bed. Because of his foresight they still continue to celebrate Wednesdays and Saturdays, not to mention the odd night covered under Section 10, Sub-Section (b).

But something has just marred the golden platter of their bliss. Where *is* her vadki?

❦

Normally Jamna's heart fluttered every Saturday. But this afternoon she lay on the bed staring sadly at the ceiling. Her mind was churning like an inferno. When Jamnadas had come home for lunch, she had hardly noticed that he had winked – an acknowledgment of it being a Saturday. He had spoken of irrelevant issues like the soaring rates at the stock-exchange, as he slurped noisily through his kadhi. After lunch he had extracted a Cavender's from his pocket and blown clouds of smoke all over the room. But no smile had appeared on Jamna's lips. Usually Jamna liked to see Jamnadas smoking. She'd say: When you wear goggles and smoke cigarettes, you look just like Ashok Kumar.

But Jamna's mind was elsewhere as she lay on the bed. She was thinking that her neighbours were solely responsible for her sorrow: and yet, how many households did she have associations with? One could easily count these on one's fingertips. There were thirty families in Badrikashram and she had dealings with only six of them.

Among the six too, it was only with Savita she had a relationship just-like-home. But she too had not been around the last two days. She had said that she was going home to her bhai-and-bhabhi's house: God only knew where she had really gone. Savita had an old and vicious enmity with her bhabhi and just two years ago she had taken a vow to never go there. So where had she gone? With whom had she gone? Whose eyes did she think she was throwing mud in? Along with the missing vadki, these questions also perturbed Jamna.

❦

It was two o'clock on Saturday afternoon. Savita had returned home just this morning so she was still busy with the household chores.

When Vimla came to meet her, she was cleaning the kitchen floor with a wet rag. Seeing Vimla at her doorstep Savita was worried, the cross-examination would soon begin.

Savita: *Vimla, you worthless woman, who are you to stand there asking questions? What have I to do with you?* Welcome Vimlaben, I was just thinking of coming over to your place after I finished the cleaning.

Vimla: I just finished my chores. Your bhai has left for office and since I hadn't seen your face for many days, I thought I'd come over.

Savita: *What's there to see in my face? Don't I know that you have come to cross-examine me?* I too was keen to meet you.

Vimla: *Liar! You'd never want to meet me! Where were you for two days? I want to know that!* How are your bhai-and-bhabhi?

Savita: *Just two days out of town and you get a stomach-ache, don't you?* If there's illness at home is it not one's duty to go? Bhabhi was unwell, so I went.

Vimla: *Rascal, you've been absconding for two days! Who have you seduced this time?* It's a woman's lot. One has to clean utensils, whether it is at one's husband's place or at one's brother's place. But how's bhabhi now?

Savita: If there's no letter in fifteen days, I'll have to go again.

Vimla: *So! She's fixed everything!* I used to ask my brother's well-being everyday.

Savita: *Don't I know that? You just love acting coy while talking to other women's husbands* He never tires of praising you. You took great care of him. *(Changing the topic ...)* Jamna had come over.

Vimla: *You changed the topic, didn't you? You cunning bitch!* Yes. Her vadki is lost.

Savita: What does she think? Am I a vadki-thief? Just three days back I'd returned her vadki – why does she come swinging her big bum to ask questions every now and again? Are all of us thieves and is she the only honest person?

Vimla: You know her nature.

Savita: I don't have to take this from her in this birth!

Vimla: She is suspicious of everyone. If anyone so much as talks to Jamnadas she comes and stands between them like a shield.
Savita: *Don't I know your doings?* Twice already she's snooped around my kitchen, and yet this morning at eight she again dropped in to coo like a koel!
Vimla: Your just-like-home relationship has lasted with Jamna because of your good nature.
Savita: Everyone in the chawl avoids her like she has rabies.
Vimla: Jamna was petty-minded right from the beginning. Just because she loses one wretched vadki, she's taken on the entire Badrikashram.
Savita: *When you'd lost your sandsi, you'd left no stone unturned to pick quarrels with "the entire Badrikashram." Daily searches, surprise-checkings and cross-examinations!* You too had inquired once-or-twice when you'd lost your sandsi.
Vimla: If it is fated that one is to have a utensil one can never lose it.
Savita: *How could you have lost it? Everyone knew that you were taking hot almond-milk for that Shivlal.* Where did you find the sandsi eventually?
Vimla: *Don't tell me you don't remember!* You were the one who tattled all over the chawl that I used to take milk and jilebis for Shivlal.
Savita: It was such a long time ago that I forgot.
Vimla: *Surely she has seduced someone. The question is who? I must find out!* God! If little Jaglo asks for a snack this afternoon I have nothing prepared and here I am, sitting and chitchatting with you.

❦

Jamna got up from the bed. She opened the drawer of her desk and took out a pencil and paper. She sharpened the pencil with a pen-knife, sat on the chair and wrote thus:
20/3. Monday: When I had taken with batata-pauva in the vadki to Savita's place in the afternoon, she was sitting on the swing stitching buttons to a pair of pajamas.
22/3. Wednesday: At 9.00 o'clock in the morning, when I had started to steam the dal to make vedhmis, Bankumasi came over and

borrowed a vadki-ful of flour. She must have been in a hurry. She did not even stay for a chat. She'd sent Tapu to return the vadki in the evening.
23/3. Thursday: Jaglo had come from Vimlaben's place to borrow the silver vadki and achmani. They had held Satyanarayan pooja in the evening. The vadki and achmani were returned at nine o'clock that night. The achmani was sparkling clean and the vadki was full of sheera.
25/3. Saturday: Vimlaben had come in the evening to borrow melvan. I gave her a spoonful. She returned the spoon the next morning.
26/3. Sunday: Savita had sent a vadki-ful of dal. According to her, that vadki was mine. Bankumasi was here when the vadki arrived. She remembers a vadki, but she does not remember what it looked like. I never use vadkis with upturned edges.
29/3. Wednesday: Savita doesn't even need a reason to pick a quarrel. When I asked her about the vadki, she had snorted. With an air of injured innocence she had asked, Do we want to make our money by stealing your vadki? Just two years ago, she had borrowed my cloth-bag to buy vegetables. What had happened then? When I had asked for the bag three-four times, hadn't she pretended as if she knew nothing about cloth-bags? Wasn't it a nightmare to recover the bag from her? The liar just loves to shove everything under her big bottom.
1/4. Saturday: Just decided. There's only one solution. I'll give five peppermints to Vimlaben's Jaglo and send him to all the five houses to check their vadkis. If it is still not found, I will personally inspect their kitchens.

❦

She tied the piece of paper at one end of her saree and lay down on the bed again. Suddenly there was a knock on the door. Think of the devil and ... It was Satan! In person. Smartly dressed. With hair styled to resemble an upturned straw broom, carrying a top in one hand and a piece of string in the other.
Jamna: I was just thinking of you.

Jaglo: *(unstrings the spinning top in his palm with a flourish)* Then you must have a job for me.
Jamna: Jagla, do you want a peppermint?
Jaglo: You only offer peppermints when you want to get something done. (*Draws an imaginary sword from an imaginary scabbard at his waist)* We are not entertained. We reject your plea. *(Abandons the imaginary hardware)* What's the job? The going rate for delivering Savitakaki's letters is one rupee a letter. The days are over when peppermints could get any real work done.
Jamna: Twenty-five paise.
Jaglo: We are not beggars. Don't even bother to mention less than fifty paise in our presence.
Jamna: To whom did you take Savita's letters?
Jaglo: One rupee for telling the name. Fixed rate. Now, what was it that you wanted?

❦

Jamna: *(rises and opens the cupboard)* I'll give you the rupee but you'll have to tell me everything. You'll get the eight annas after you do my job.
Jaglo: *(pockets the rupee)* Last week I'd gone to Vithal Sadan across the street to hand over her letter to Shantilal. We have our ethics. I've not told anyone else about this. Now, what's your assignment?
Jamna: See. I'll write down the names of five families in our chawl. All you have to do is to go to their kitchens and check the names inscribed on all their vadkis. Then come back and tell me if the name on any vadki is Jamnadas Bapalal.
Jaglo: This is a lot of work. The minimum charge for this assignment is one rupee. I'll have to take the kids from all these houses into confidence.
Jamna: Okay. You'll get a rupee. But I need to know this by the 2nd. *So, Savita has started a correspondence with Shantilal! It wouldn't surprise me if he was the one she was with the last couple of days. The minute Shantilal's wife left for her mother's place to have her*

baby there, Savita has gone and infiltrated the household. One never knows about the human heart – who'll fall in love with whom and fall out of love too.

Every Saturday night, Jamna burnt incense, lit perfumed agarbattis in three corners, wore a veni in her hair, cooked dal-dhokli for supper and switched off the lights early. Saturday and Wednesday nights Jamnadas did not go to have his smoke in the verandah with the menfolk of Badrikashram.

Today, when Jamnadas sat for dinner, there was no dal-dhokli. From the time they got married, the fixed menu for every Saturday night was dal-dhokli and for every Wednesday night, vedhmi. Jamna would add extra leaven in the dhokli to make it soft as pooris. She would spread several teaspoons of ghee on the vedhmi and serve it enthusiastically, often cajoling him to eat more than he wanted to. Today there was no enthusiasm, no cajoling, no love. Jamnadas ate hastily, eyes downcast. He washed his hands and, while chopping betelnuts, he finally began the conversation.

Jamnadas: What's the matter? Why do you look so upset? (*Without uttering a word Jamna went to the sink to put away the dishes.*)

Jamnadas: I say, why are you angry with me? Have you forgotten today is Saturday?

Jamna: Who says I am angry with you?

Jamnadas: Then why was I punished with gourd-and-potato vegetable? Is it not the day for dal-dhokli?

Jamna: I know what day it is.

Jamnadas: You know very well that I can't stand this sickly gourd-and-potato.

Jamna: When I put away the dishes I noticed that you had not even touched it.

Jamnadas: Then what's the matter with you?

Jamna: Go ask your neighbours of Badrikashram. They have not spared me any sorrow.

Jamnadas: What happened?
Jamna: Ask me what has not happened!
Jamnadas: Consider it asked.
Jamna: You remember, we went to buy a set of stainless steel vadkis on dhanteras five years ago?
Jamnadas: When was that?
Jamna: When Nitu was born at Motabhai's house. That year you had fractured your hand during Navratri. The same year, on dhanteras we had bought a set of six vadkis for eighty rupees.
Jamnadas: So what about them?
Jamna: Well, I can't find one vadki of that set.
Jamnadas: Never mind, we will buy a new one.
Jamna: Such sets are not available anymore.
Jamnadas: We'll buy a better set. Don't worry yourself over it.
Jamna: So if someone swallows our vadkis, we're supposed to just run out and buy a new set, is it? I want the same vadki and I want to find out who has stolen it.
Jamnadas: You go on breaking you head over it. I will not interfere. Let me know when you want a new set

Jamnadas made a pan and placed it in his cheek. He then sat for half an hour in the verandah. That night both of them slept with their backs to each other. Jamna lay awake for some time thinking that a woman who could steal somebody's husband would not be ashamed to steal a vadki.

❦

On the evening of the 2nd, Jaglo arrived with disastrous news. He reported that he had thoroughly investigated all the five families listed. None of the kitchens had a vadki with *Jamnalal Bapalal* inscribed on it. Jaglo asked for a hike in his fees. One and a half rupees. In four of the houses he had to use bribes of upto four peppermints to get the job done by his friends. This assignment had proved to be a total loss for him. Should Jamna not give him the one and a half rupees at once, then he would be compelled to write *Savita Vadkichor* on the walls of

Badrikashram. Since everyone in the chawl knew that it was Jamna who had recently lost a vadki, she would be prime suspect as the sponsor such a campaign. This would only give Jamna a bad name. But Jamna had the tact to convert any situation to her advantage. She played with one and a half rupees in her palm and said, "I will give you the money. You have worked for it. But you will have to tell me where Savita and Shantilal meet."

Jaglo's eyes were rivetted to the coins. "While returning from the evening darshan they meet in the garden of Madhavbagh." Having said this, he put the coins in his pocket and left.

Jamna began to think. She remembered that when she had gone to give batata-pauva to Savita, she was stitching buttons on a pair of pajamas. Savita's husband always wore a dhoti and her kids always wore half-pants. Surely the pajamas must be Shantilal's. Then she remembered the conversation she had had when she had met Savita that evening.

Savita: I am never able to cook such soft batata-pauva.

Jamna: *If you are a miser with oil what else do you expect?* There is nothing to it. Everyone cooks this way. Don't flatter me unnecessarily.

Savita: So I may be flattering you unnecessarily, but why would Shantilal lie in such a small matter?

Jamna: Shantilal?

Savita: The one who lives in that grand flat in Vithal Sadan across the street.

If the vadki had reached Shantilal's house, Jamna felt she would never get it back. Jamna thought it over for the twenty-second time. When Bankumasi had come over to borrow the flour, her eyes were moist. She had not even stayed back to chat for a couple of minutes. The poor, unhappy woman! Her husband beat her up regularly for no fault of hers. Yet she was so considerate! That every evening her son Tapu returned the flour in the same vadki. Even his face was lacklustre. He had not even stopped to taste the freshly cooked vedhmi filling.

On the evening of the 25th Vimlaben had come to borrow some melvan. She had stayed back to gossip.

Vimla: Your vadki must be at Savita's place.

Jamna: I've been there twice. The house was locked.
Vimla: She was saying that her bhai and bhabhi have called her over.
Jamna: How can that be? She does not get along with her bhabhi at all.
Vimla: Then where do you think she has gone?
Jamna: You can never tell with her. She aims at one targets and scores a bull's eye on another.
Vimla: When my sandsi was lost, remember all that happened afterwards? I had to lift hot pots of vegetable, milk and rice with a rag. Ten days later, it was found at Shivlalbhai's house.
Jamna: *The whole town knows how crazy you are about Shivlal.* Is that so? Had you found it at Shivlalbhai's place? I had simply forgotten.
Vimla: *You are no less than Savita.* It's been over two years. That is why you forgot. Remember, you'd sent the silver vadki and achmani to my place on the day of the Satyanarayan pooja?
Jamna: I also remember that you had taken the trouble to return the vessels filled with prasad. Why, you even returned the melvan spoon. In the last month I have not even sent the tiffin to anyone. See there it sits and yawns.
Vimla: Savita is very careless by nature.
Jamna: Her intentions are not good. It was a pain to get my cloth bag back from her. I had sent the vadki with the batata-pauva. Now it has gone directly to Shantilal's house. We'll never get it back.
Vimla: Shantilal?
Jamna: I don't know him. Savita was saying, he has a grand flat across the street on the first floor of Vithal Sadan.
Vimla: Yes, I have seen him. Savita is too much. She can bring down a flying bird. We would not even notice the bird.
Jamna: I still don't know anything about Shantilal. But it is a fact that in front of your brother she likes to dress up and simper.

❦

On Sunday the 2nd, Jamna sat watching *Ramayana* with a view to follow the adventures of the ideal woman. But Jamnadas observed that her eyes would often stray towards the door. Just as Ram assembled his army of monkeys on the opposite shores of Ravan's Lanka, Vimlaben dropped in. She signalled to Jamna who slithered out of the room so as to not disturb Jamnadas.

Vimla: She had just come over to leave her key at my place.

Jamna: Did she say anything?

Vimla: No. Her Highness was in full regalia. Chiffon saree, lipstick and reeking of perfume. When she handed over the key to me, she looked like a fragrant honeycomb.

Jamna: Where has she gone! When will she return?

Vimla: She has gone over to Shantilal's to watch *Ramayana* on his colour television. So she will be back when it is over at 10.15.

Jamna: Such dressing up just to go across the street?

Vimla: She has gone to throw mud in Shantilal' eyes.

Jamna: Then let us get it over with.

Vimla: I will keep a watch near the parapet. If anyone comes your way I will cough three times.

Jamna: And I will come out immediately.

Vimla: Take care though that no one notices you.

❦

Jamna opened the lock to Savita's house and entered. She started with the kitchen. Shelves, sinks, pots, pans, oil containers, the ghee vadki, the grain bin – inside, outside, everywhere. Around none of this could she find the vadki bearing Jamnadas' name inscribed on it. In the living room she examined the table, the chair, the lamp, the book, the file, the wrist watch, the carpet, the double-bed and the table fan. Disappointment here too. She searched the store room, the bathroom, the latrine all over. Half-an-hour later when she emerged, Jamna looked like a sadhu, a layer of ash on her face.

Vimla: Who are you?

Jamna: It's me.

Vimla: What is this you have done to your face?

Jamna: The whole house is covered with dust. If she had any time

left from wondering all over town only then would she find time to take care of her own house. The stray bitch!
Vimla: Did you find it?
Jamna: No.
Vimla: She may have hidden it somewhere.
Jamna: I went through every corner of her house with a tooth comb. My vadki is not in this house.
Vimla: Come along. It is time we left, she will be here any moment like an angel of death.

❦

Sunday evening was also the same – Jamna lay defeated on the bed staring vacantly at the white ceiling. Jamnadas could not bear to see her so unhappy. He sat on the bed and took Jamna's head in his lap.
Jamnadas: Why do you torture yourself? If the vadki has gone we'll buy a new one. Why do you worry your precious self over this trivial matter and make me so unhappy?
Jamna: Do I complain if they eat our soft-soft batata-pauva? But I simply cannot bear anyone devouring the vadki with it. I don't want to live in Badrikashram any more. Find us rooms in another chawl.
Jamnadas: There will be neighbours in every chawl, and you'll feel lonely in a flat.

Jamnadas got up from the bed and brought a glass of water for Jamna. She refused it with a shake of her head. He switched on the television because it was time for the Sunday feature film. It was an Ashok Kumar film. If any other day, Jamna had known of an Ashok Kumar film, she would have served dinner right in front of the television set. Nothing diverts her from her grief today, thought Jamnadas as he watched the film distractedly.

In the film a nautch girl dances and signs. Pretending to be drunk, Ashok Kumar sidles up to her. The girl surreptitiously slips something in his palm and whispers in his ear. He staggers out. When he reaches the ground floor Ashok Kumar straightens up, abandons his pretense and knocks on a door. He passes the object to someone inside and walks away.

Watching this, Jamnadas started. He leaped up from his chair as if a scorpion had bitten him. He put on his chappals and ran down the staircase two steps at a time just like Jaglo. He reached the ground floor and knocked on Shivlal's door. The door opened. Shivlal's hair was dyed a deep black.

Shivlal: Welcome! Why did you leave the film halfway through?

Jamnadas: Shivlal! I was given a choice. Either to see the film or to see Jamna's funeral!

Shivlal: Whatever happened?

Jamnadas: She is on hunger strike.

Shivlal: Good for her. She needs to lose weight.

Jamnadas: Here I am so troubled and you want to tease me!

Shivlal: Unless you tell me how will I know what is bothering you?

Jamnadas: Do you remember – last week you needed some oil when you were making chappattis?

Shivlal: So?

Jamnadas: I'd brought it with me when I'd come to sit in the verandah.

Shivlal: I remember. That night Jamna had gone to do the garba.

Jamnadas: Well, that vadki is lost.

Shivlal: But it must be right here. Sit down, I'll find it.

Shivlal went to the kitchen and started knocking pots and pans around to search for the vadki.

Jamnadas: Have you found it?

Shivlal: I am looking.

Jamnadas: If you can't find it the world will end.

Shivlal: The vadki must surely be at Vimla's place. I will ask her to take it to your place tomorrow.

When Jamnadas returned, the television was on and Jamna was fast asleep.

❦

On the afternoon of Monday, the 3rd April, while sipping his butter-

milk, Jamnadas asked with studied casualness :
Jamnadas: So what happened to that vadki? Could you find it.
Jamna: Vimlaben returned it this morning.
Jamnadas: Now you must be relieved.
Jamna: What relief?
Jamnadas: Why, what happened?
Jamna: It would have been better if I had not found the vadki.
Jamnadas: What went wrong?
Jamna: It was found at Shivlal's place.
Jamnadas: How?
Jamna: Who knows how it ended up there? I can't stand the sight of the man. The way he speaks, with emphasis on every word, that sophisticated whisper of his and that ghastly dye in his hair. I feel like slapping him.
Jamnadas: The fellow seems okay to me.
Jamna: You are really naive. Vimla would not hesitate to set fire to her own house over him. Get the message?
Jamnadas: Why?
Jamna: Vimla will now feel that now I have a special relationship with Shivlal. If the vadki had not been found I would not be the target of such suspicion.
Jamnadas: Have I accused you of anything?
Jamna: I will have to get at the bottom of this. How did the vadki reach there?
Jamnadas: Forget it. We found the vadki. It is enough.
Jamna: Your wish is my command.

❦

Jamnadas heaved a sigh of relief.

IDEAS, COLOURS, COMPOSITIONS

A Statement

1. When I reflect on the East-West Visual Arts Encounter, the striking features that come to my mind are the room where the discussions were held, and the open maidan where all the artists did their paintings. In the maidan, the wind blew angrily, the sea roared, and people looked at us through the grills of the building of National Centre for the Performing Arts.

2. Never had I encountered so many artists speaking, explaining, exploring in totally different visual languages.

I heard about:

a. An artist who gathers pollen, puts it in bottles, and then spreads it on the floor. Brass thalis on the floor for Brahma Bhojan!
b. An artist concerned with light passing through a prism.
c. A village background and first lessons in the alphabet.
d. Anti-nuclear propositions, the decadence of the West and the need for a white revolution.
e. The Shiv-Shakti spirit in Tantric teachings.
f. Basic and fundamental courses for first-year college students.
g. Sermons to Indian artists that they should be inspired by folk art and traditional paintings.

3. From the Western artists, prophecies were uttered about the future of humanity.

4. I accept the self and the ego which govern the artist. They are the driving forces for him to create his work. Very few artists have an objective view about the work of other artists. They are so involved in their own work that it does not allow them to appreciate a totally different point of view. During the seminar many points of view were thrown at us.

5. Artists whose work I liked somehow made me feel its validity. The validity of the idea originates in the work.

6. Like a thief, an artist steals ideas, colours, compositions from other artists' works. Then he changes them and mixes them with his own.

This Staetment is an extract from *ARTISTS TODAY : EAST -WEST VISUAL ARTS ENCOUNTER* edited by Ursula Bickelmann & Nissim Ezekiel, Marg Publications, Bombay 1987. *The Visual Arts Encounter* was held in Bombay from February 8 - 14, 1995. Sponsored by the National Centre for the Performing Arts and the Max Mueller Bhavan, *Encounter* was part of the project that called for meetings in the fields of music, dance, science and philosophy.

7. I remember vividly. One particular discussion This was about how Indian artists (as a group) do not react to political events, riots, the tragedy in Bhopal. I accept my failure in that context.

8. The fact that India has a living tradition and yet most Indian painters look towards the West for their inspiration infuriated many Indian artists. The question remains open for me. The situation in Indian classical dance is not to be envied. Tourists find the "real" India in these dances as they do in "snake charmers." It is exportable. Contemporary Indian painters have made an attempt to reject this perception, to fuse Western and Eastern traditions. They have tried.

9. It is surprising that though so many artists were present, there were no "fights." Artists behaved almost like gentlemen. Towards the end, an attempt was made to provoke Indian artists. This was done by mentioning the names of Indian artists whose works, a Western artist considered, did not reflect a primary understanding of design.

The anger of Indian painters who were included in this group was fascinating to note.

10. There is a parable written by Kahlil Gibran. An atheist and a believer meet. For days they discuss questions about the existence of God or His non-existence. After a week, they separate. The atheist becomes a theist and the theist an atheist! It would be quite amusing if all my Western artist friends start painting in the style of the Indian miniatures! And if Matisse or Picasso inspired only Indian artists!

The Crafting Years

1934 Born on March 10th in Bombay.

1961 He gives up a career in chartered accountancy and joins the Faculty of Fine Arts, M S University in Baroda for an MA in Art Criticism.

1965 He has his first exhibition at the Jehangir Art Gallery, Bombay. Also begins publishing stories in Gujarati.

1966 He is featured in George Butcher's *Selection of Indian Art* shown in England. He participates in group shows of Baroda artists in Ahmedabad, and *Art Now in India Exhibition* held in London, New Castle and Ghent.

1968 He wins an honourable mention in the *First Triennale*, India. Also participates in the *Sao Paulo Biennale* and a group show in Switzerland.

1969 He takes on the joint editorship of *Vrischik*, an art magazine for three years.

1975 He is sponsored by the British Council Division to visit UK. He participates in the *Third Triennale*, Menton

1976 He travels to the USSR and Yugoslavia under the Department of Educational Exchange Programme. He exhibits at London and is included in the *Narrative Painting Exhibition* by Timothy Hyman.

1979 He teaches at the Bath Academy, Corsham, U K.

1982 His work is shown along with that of six other artists at the Tate Gallery by Howard Hodgkin.

1984 The Padma Shri is conferred on him.

1991 His play, *Mojila Manilal* is published by Sahacharya Prakashan as a special issue of *Gadyaparva*.

1992 He receives the Katha Award for Creative Fiction for the short story, "Pages From a Diary."

1995 The National Portrait Gallery, Britain buys his portrait of Salman Rushdie for £10,000.

Krishna [signature]

KRISHNA SOBTI

"I see in myself a person who takes life directly and touches life indirectly."
– Krishna Sobti

The need to reach the core of a matter, to unravel its deepest secrets, and then explicate the intricacies of that issue in actual lived and experienced terms, is what has prompted Krishna Sobti to produce one exciting, innovative, controversial work after another. Her writings invariably manage to stir the proverbial hornet's nest and agitate both the doyens and keepers of literary criticism as well the more ordinary, but nevertheless discerning reader. Which is perhaps why Krishna Sobti never lets herself forget that she is ultimately responsible only to herself and her readers.

Krishna Sobti was born on February 18, 1925 in Gujarat (West

Punjab, now in Pakistan) and was brought up in New Delhi – a city she is quite passionate about! "New Delhi holds a certain mystique for me. Culturally, it decided the framework I operate in. It gave me a vital view of things, people and happenings." Though a "real Delhiwallah," she feels that her ancestral home in West Punjab was a perfect foil for Delhi. "These two opposites created a rich fund of reality."

Little wonder then that Sobti claims that her "intellectual and creative responses are deeply rooted in an eclectic integrated cultural system." She consistently refuses to look at her historical background through any particular received perception that feeds and projects a specific ideology. "Official history" has no meaning for her as far as it excludes "history from below." The most significant political event of her generation was the Partition, and the irreversible and irrevocable drama of the communal divide was a lived reality for Krishna Sobti.

Memories of an idyllic childhood spent in the ancestral haveli at Gujarat alternated by life in Delhi, Shimla and Lahore were lost in the horrific drama of the Partition. "We were told that Muslims had turned us out of their new homeland. We also saw that we too pushed Muslims to the other side ... Common people created a living mythology – a shade better than the so-called official history. It did assume the sanctity of the shared past, with its human connections of political nature." Out of this mythology was born the Sahitya Akademi Award-winning *Zindaginama*. A chronicle of the Partition, the novel is suffused with ethos and ambience of pre-partition rural Punjab. She recalls, "Khwaja Khizr, the Pir of Zindaginama, was a living symbol for all peasants. He was their special guardian. If this was a myth, it was one that all faiths cherished deeply."

As for her personal history, Krishna Sobti says she is "a writer who happens to be a liberal, middle-class woman. I need to have my freedom so that my creative apparatus functions smoothly." It seems there never was a time when she did not want to be a writer. And her first story "Lama," was the result of a long-abiding fascination with a Tibetan lama and the need to articulate this.

"I find it boring to continue in the same vein, vocabulary and vision," Sobti says, providing a perfect description of her literary history. The writer in her changes persona according to the needs of characters and situations. Mere imagination has no role here, the writer has to be able to look outside herself and listen closely to all the footfalls and echoes around her. For her, the benchmark of success is that her characters should ring true to themselves.

A writer who had the proofs of her first novel – a five-hundred-page saga – destroyed because the changes made by the proof reader were "not true to the lives I was portraying," Krishna Sobti is most eloquent on the subject of language. "I confront, I discover, I define and redefine with the help of language" – these are just some of the demands she makes of it! It is this which caused the editors of the authoritative *Women Writing in India* to throw up their hands in despair while trying to get a representative selection of her work translated. As they said, "standard forms of English, sanitized as they have been over the last two hundred years, just did not stretch into anything that resembled the scope of Sobti's idiom."

And Krishna Sobti's language resources seem limitless – from the earthy flavour of rural Punjab to the uninhibited sexual bantering of *Mitro Marjani* and the purani Dilli ethos of *Dil-o-Danish* – all these are delineated with an effortless honesty all her own. Besides, it is a double offering for it is not just as she Sobti that she speaks, but also as Hashmat.

One fine day, nearly twenty years ago, Sobti met Hashmat. Pen-name, spiritual double, intellectual rival and alter ego, Hashmat miyan usurped her place at the writing table. Not for long, fortunately. The uneasy barrier soon dropped and the two assumed a comfortable friendship. "We both have different identities," she explains. "I protect, and he reveals; I am ancient, he is new and fresh; we operate from opposite directions." Hashmat became a chronicler of a different kind, of the bohemian 1960s and 70s, and of the coffee-house culture. Even here, Sobti remained an observer as well as a participant. Which is why, she can say authoritatively, "It is a circuit game barred to outsiders."

Amidst this mad bustle of activity, lobbying manouvres, rush for awards and efforts to chair committees, Sobti has carefully distanced herself in order to preserve her identity and integrity as a writer and a writer alone. "You can take liberties with yourself only if you create a large space for yourself, a vast sky." And without doubt, Sobti-Hashmat has done just that.

Ultimately Sobti stays in our minds as a gutsy, indomitable woman who likes to live on her own and who – as a writer and as an individual – has created a niche for herself in Hindi literature that is rightfully hers. But much more than that, she is the kind of person who can sustain a solitary court ordeal over thirteen years to uphold a principle, someone who giggles as merrily as a schoolgirl while relegating herself to "senior citizen" status, someone anyone can relate to. A special person.

KRISHNA SOBTI

in conversation with
Tarun Bhartiya &
Jayeeta Sharma

I fell in love with her. Maybe I have something going for short women in sparkling turquoise salwar kameezes. Wait till she reads that – saala sara maza kharaab kar diya. *But maybe not. Hashmat might decide to take over from Sobti and a text on the interview(ers) shall pour forth, ruminating on everything which went into the making of this interview – the tea, the biscuits and grapes that we appropriated, or the texture of my shirt and my language, the number of stairs she had to climb to get some namkeen for us ... But are you going to tell us something useful about her or not? the editor moans ... All right, you asked for an interview, we got you two – one with Sobti's alter ego*

Hashmat also! When biography is called upon to illuminate literature then you hear opinions, if opinions are aired to illustrate worldviews then you share anecdotes, and if sharing anecdotes allows intimacy then you hear the spontaneous laughter, the joie de vivre of one who takes the world and herself lightly ... Now, what is this? Nothing really, just intimations of an interview which did not take place. So what did you do? Nothing. KRISHNA SOBTI HAPPENED. That's all.

***TB:** We heard that you were quite a presence at the Women's Studies Conference at Jaipur last week – the participants were absolutely charmed by the flowers you bought them. What was your experience of it?*

KS: Normally, I keep away from such events, in fact, this was one of the few times I had been to a women's conference, but I found it very stimulating. All those young women there, the way everything had been organized, the quality of the discussions. I respond keenly to certain kinds of confidence and freshness ... the only way I could express my admiration was by just getting a rose for each one there ... the vivaciousness of those young women, their energy, the way they ran around if I needed a plate or something, I felt my steps were dragging. I had to tell myself I'm not a hundred yet.

THOSE YOUNG WOMEN, THEIR ENERGY ... I HAD TO TELL MYSELF I'M NOT A HUNDRED YET.

***JS:** What kind of framework would you put yourself in – as a person, as a woman, and as a writer?*

KS: I have always been my own person. It is easier to exaggerate or simplify the difference between people. My biological history says I am a woman. History and individuals cannot ignore each other. A writer must be autonomous, a free individual. I believe that our individuality embraces our innermost uniqueness. And this individuality could be qualitatively different from person to person, not necessarily from male to female.

I am a writer who happens to be a liberal, middle-class woman. I need to have my freedom so that my creative apparatus functions smoothly. I see in myself a creative writer who has a total commitment to her creativity and art.

***JS:** Could you tell us a little about this liberal middle-class background?*

KS: I think the best thing that ever happened to me was that I was brought up in *New* Delhi. It was a small place then, but a very open one. We would spend six months of the year here and the other six in Shimla. We used to play hockey in the Talkatora Gardens. But interaction with my village never stopped and these two opposites created a rich fund of reality.

Ours was not a joint family – this was unusual for those times. In fact, our interaction with the relatives was very formal, very correct. I had three sisters and a brother. My father was a stickler for discipline. He would insist that we go to bed by 9.30 pm – I flout that now, I start work at 10.00 pm! He used to read stories to us every night. My mother was a strong woman, very pragmatic – she had what I call a "peasant temperament." She was married at eighteen. I never saw her give in to anyone. I was free to do anything as long as I could convince her of my reasons for doing it.

One particular incident left a great impression on me. We were at our haveli in Gujarat (now in West Pakistan). A small fortress built of little bricks, children were not allowed to go to the cellars. I told my mother once, "I want to go into the cellars." She said, "Go. Can anyone stop you if you really want to?" I hesitated, recalling all the horror stories I had heard about them. I still remember distinctly what she had said then. "You have to choose – you can either see what the cellars are like, or you can keep being scared of the snakes there." She taught us to never complain about anything – I still don't. I wrote *Ai Ladki* after her death. She could have climbed Mount Everest had the circumstances been different! I think I have inherited my matter-of-factness from her. My father was the reflective one.

Did I tell you Sobti is derived from the Greek "Sofitus"? Once, Dr Nihar Ranjan Ray told me about a Greek coin with *Sobti* inscribed on it in Devanagari on one side and *Sofitus* on the other. My family used to follow a few customs which were probably Greek in origin. For instance, before any special event, a tray full of mutton would be left in the open. We would go ahead with the celebration only after this had been taken away by a kite. I have always been fascinated by history. My family had in its possession the bric-à-brac of the Third Sikh War! The difference between officially-documented history and history, as seen from below, is incredible. It lives through the collective consciousness of the people.

JS: *Wasn't it this interest in history which shaped your magnum opus* – Zindaginama?

KS: Yes. It took me almost three decades to write those words. But I am very patient. I can wait endlessly.

TB: *Three decades!*

KS: Hmm ... In 1952, I sent a six-hundred-page manuscript to Bharati Bhandar Press in Allahabad. I had been publishing stories since 1944 but this was my first novel, *Channa*. The manuscript was accepted, but when I saw the proofs, I noticed that many words had been substituted – "Shahni" was changed to "Shahpatni" and so on. They probably wanted to improve what they thought was my inability to write standard Hindi. I went to Allahabad at once, since I felt that these changes were not true to the lives I was portraying. Half the forms for a four-thousand print run had already been printed. The publishers did not take my objections seriously. After a

THE BEST THING THAT EVER HAPPENED TO ME WAS THAT I WAS BROUGHT UP IN *NEW* DELHI.

number of meetings I convinced them to destroy the proofs at my cost. All I asked for was to be allowed to pay in two instalments!

Some people, who had read an extract in *Prateek,* asked me for the manuscript. By then I had looked at it again and did not consider it good enough yet to be published. So I put it away. I took it out after five years but again I put it aside. Finally, Sheela Sandhu of Rajkamal – my publishers – came with a request to rework the manuscript. I told her that the paper was too brittle, as an excuse. She had it promptly retyped and back on my table!

***JS:** Did you go to a college in Delhi?*

KS: No. I was at Fatehchand College in Lahore – I did not make the grade for the prestigious Kennott College. I had a great time in Lahore. We went for moonlight picnics and jaunts on our cycles. With the Partition we lost our holdings in West Punjab. Meanwhile, I had taken up the job of a governess in Mount Abu.

***JS:** When did you decide to be a writer?*

KS: I never considered the prospect of not writing. I don't have any other skills, you know. No, I think there was any time when I was *not* a writer. I always felt like one. Even as a child I wanted to find rhymes for the noise of the rain, of trains and trees, the mountains ... I can clearly recall the way I used to watch a Tibetan lama's impersonal face. I wanted to paint that unusual face but could never do it the way I wanted to. Finally, I wrote a story titled "Lama" – my first. This and my next story, "Nafisa" were published by *Vichar,* a leading literary journal of the day.

***JS:** Could you tell us a little about all those years when you were both writing and working at a full-time job as an editor in the Adult Literacy Department of the Delhi Administration?*

KS: I worked there for quite some time. I had fixed up a taxi which would collect me at ten every morning to take me to work. In the evening that taxi would bring me home via Connaught Place. I used to roam about a lot then, spend a lot of time with friends at restaurants. After a bath and a drink, I would settle down to work and continue till about 3.30 am. Then sleep till nine and be off to work at ten. I gave up the job in 1980 to make more time for my writing.

***JS:** What are your writing habits like now?*

KS: I sit at my table at about ten at night. I continue till about 4.30 am. Then I go to bed. I'm not really myself during the daytime. I don't know what's going on. *(She asked us to call only at night for further appointments. She is famous, we heard, for the calls she makes just before she goes to bed at 5.30 am!)*

Each time I go to the table I like to begin afresh. My earlier efforts are of no help. I only need clues from the first line and build from there. If you try to control the text, then you are not allowing it the space or strength to grow.

I am a slow-speed woman. I keep on absorbing things and use them when they have matured enough. Sometimes your language fails, it makes you realize your limitations. I work on three drafts. The first is the authoritative one. I don't consult it when I'm doing the next two drafts. I look at the text critically in the second draft. Then I do the third draft like the first and compare the two. Usually there are very few differences.

I NEVER CONSIDERED THE PROSPECT OF NOT WRITING. I DON'T HAVE ANY OTHER SKILLS, YOU KNOW.

***B:** Why do you go through three drafts then?*

KS: For the silent text, the text behind the text! The third draft tells you whether you have been good or not. If the silent text is still verbal, it really bothers me. There *has* to be a silent text for my readers so that they can feel the story in their gut.

***JS:** Have you always made three drafts or did this habit evolve over time?*

KS: It started with *Daar se Bichhudi*, my first novel. After I had written it, I was wondering if I should rewrite all of it just to feel that I had written a novel. I did write it again because I wanted to send the manuscript to Dharamveer Bharati's journal, *Nikash,* and did not have typing facilities. Later, even after I started getting my work typed, I realized that I would still have three drafts! I hate the sight of crossed-out lines. It disturbs me, it affects the straightness of my lines. I'd rather rewrite the lines than correct them on paper. If something goes wrong I just tear the sheet. It's easy to do that. I end up wasting a lot of paper.

When I'm in the process of writing, once I have finished a night's work, I don't allow myself to think about it all day. But I reread all of it when I go back to the table at night. I had to read at least three chapters of *Zindaginama* every night for a while! It was very boring but it had to be done. Writing is hard labour!

While at work, I restrain myself from indulging in any particular situation or character. I find that with every new book, my language changes in texture, in tonal quality. I am also particular about not meeting the "wrong" people when I'm in the process of finishing a text. But then, as I told you, I need to take it off my mind during the day. Washing utensils is my favourite way of doing that – it reduces thinking to a bare minimum. Or I read shikaar stories. I love them. Or even cook mutton. Add all the right masalas. Make it perfect, as if I won't be cooking again for the next ten years. The process of writing is such a cerebral one that you have to make it a little physical too, to balance it. Anyway, writing is not my only priority. I want to live life. I want to have fun.

***JS:** Have you ever encountered what they call writer's block?*

KS: When I am writing too easily, I feel uneasy, suspicious. Sometimes I have to remove myself from the work at hand and change my environment. I usually go off to the hills for ten, fifteen days, then come back and pick it up from where I had left off. Whenever I get stuck, I know I am in for an expensive outing!

***TB:** Does the blank page cause you any anxieties?*

KS: No, it gives me the most fantastic feeling possible! Nothing compares with that sensation ... It's as if you are on a mountain peak, with all this clear space before you. That s the mystique of a blank page.

My father used to get me really good paper. Since then I have spent a fortune on paper. There was a time when I would buy Sunlight Bond paper for Rs 5. I have to pay Rs 120 for it now. I have always used black ink and a Sheaffer or Parker pen. My first Parker was a birthday present from Bhagwati Charan Verma and the Sheaffer I have now was given to me by my father when I had my first story published. Of course, I am trying to write with these thick senior citizen pens these days ... *(laughing)* I can't read the fine print too well now.

JS: *What makes you write, Krishnaji?*

KS: My intellectual and creative responses have been deeply rooted to an eclectic and integrated human experience. I have always been conscious of two distinct elements merging in me. I believe in the concept of Ardhanariswar – both male and female elements are combined creatively in content, language, style and imagination.

I confront, I discover, I define and redefine with the help of language. A good piece is not only the result of memory and imagination woven with words, it is invariably the outcome of a complex process of intellectual and emotional intimacy with the subject. Language does create a vibrant living experience with ideas, sounds, characters, conflicts, love, hate and violence.

WRITING IS SUCH HARD LABOUR! ... WHEN I AM WRITING TOO EASILY, I FEEL UNEASY, SUSPICIOUS

Writing, for me, is the main activity of my life, not an alternative. In spite of this, I have not written anything in reaction. If I am sad, angry or happy, I do not go near my writing. My inner disposition is not so dramatic. I have a slow, set rhythm of living. When the words come, then it is a happening! It can make any demand on me. But once the writing is done, you, as the writer, are excluded from the text. Only the signature remains. I've never written in reaction. If I'm sad or angry I do a hundred other things but I write only when I have something to say. Besides, no tragedy is tragedy enough to make you lose your head. It's a matter of your reserves. Of course, every writer, every individual is made differently.

If my mind is absolutely clear, then I can't write. If you know everything then what is the use? Exploration gives you an excuse to write. I have seen the aristocracy at such close quarters – I was a governess in that small state in Mount Abu for a while – but I never wrote about it. Then I saw this young woman in Rajasthan once and the image stayed in my mind. I was charmed and moved. She intrigued me. Years later, one afternoon, I saw a room with a skylight and an old man lying on a charpai. The opening scene of *Mitro Marjani* came years later, in Delhi, easily and quietly. The Rajasthani woman in a lehenga, carrying bricks on her head, came alive.

JS: *That's probably your most discussed work – What else went into the making of it?*

KS: Oh, I gave the old man three sons and then gave wives to the sons. I even put in a married daughter who comes to her parents' home for a visit. Though I wasn't equipped to handle a joint family since I've never lived in one, I settled for a large one, thinking, "*I* don't have to give birth to all these people, so why not have a large family anyway?"

Mitro Marjani was not a writer's story. It was Mitro's story. I was amazed at the surprises she gave me at every turn. Like when she asks her sister-in-law, "Have you ever seen such breasts?" It was the New Woman revelling in her physicality. Yaar, I was impressed with her! She had no inhibitions talking about things tabooed by tradition – to express pleasure in sex. Her defiance was of a kind I could not ignore.

TB: *But you sent her back to her husband at the end of the book – wasn't that a rather tame way to end Mitro's story?*

KS: Feminists have criticized the book for just that. But I feel that she would need to be educated first, to be more discriminating. To me she seems to show remarkable sense in the context of her circumstances. I have no reasons to be unhappy with the choice she makes ultimately.

***JS:** A trivial question now – how do you arrive at your titles?*

KS: There really is no fixed formula for that. I usually name a work after it is complete. When I finished writing what ultimately became *Yaaron ke Yaar,* I couldn't come up with a name for it for almost a week. But one day, in my sleep, though I don't normally dream much, I saw myself walking along Janpath past the signboard of a shop that read *Yaaron ke Yaar* – and there, I had the title.

***TB:** You did not let your first novel be published because of changes made in the language. But your language keeps changing from work to work – take your most recent books* Dil-O-Danish *and* Ai Ladki *for instance?*

KS: A work is an organic whole and each work makes different demands on the writer in terms of style and language. A language is nothing if it doesn't convey a certain sensibility. My strength is that I have an apparatus which enables me to receive things from many directions. While writing *Zindaginama*, I was surprised at how one's memory banks words – language is what one has imbibed, assimilated through life. I was completely under the dictates of a certain period. And my effort was to capture the thrust of the spoken word. *Dil-O-Danish* was about Delhi – very different from *Ai Ladki* which is a very "writerly" book. In fact, it's present form is the result of my inability to write it as a play.

MITRO MARJANI WAS NOT A WRITER'S STORY. IT WAS MITRO'S STORY. I WAS AMAZED AT THE SURPRISES SHE GAVE ME AT EVERY TURN.

JS: *You said that Ai Ladki was written after your mother's death. Is it an autobiographical work?*

KS: Not after a point. When my mother was in the Intensive Care Unit, she kept repeating the line, "The light will keep burning." This line stayed in my head and led to *Ai Ladki*. What is strange is that the line which inspired the work is not in it!

TB: *What is your creed as a writer?*

KS: I take my readers very, very seriously. I believe that if you distort anything while writing, you are destroying the trust reposed in you. You have to be terribly honest because you are writing for all those people who read you because they can't write themselves. You can't indulge your emotions or you will be sentimental. And you cannot give your readers half-truths.

JS: *Do you read the works of other writers?*

KS: I read things en bloc – you can know something, learn from it only if you read all of it. Once I found myself fascinated by Napoleon and I read everything about him that I could lay my hands on, even *Desiree* which was made into a film with Marlon Brando. I read all of Phanishwar Nath Renu's work since I had to present a paper on him. It was difficult reading at first. Then I started reading aloud and realized the kind of effect he creates with sounds!

Reading other writers has helped me know my limitations, to recognize work that is not good enough. Half-hearted efforts won't do in literature. You have to have the stamina to give it all you have, and the strength to accept failure – it's terrible when literary efforts fail.

JS: *Who are your favourite writers, Krishnaji?*

KS: Tolstoy, in fiction. The worldview he presents in his work is very close to the way he lived, and that is something I admire. I used to be very enthusiastic about Lawrence Durrell, his *Alexandria Quartet*, till someone informed me that Durrell was considered to be "colonial" in his orientation. I reread his work and I still like his style. I've just finished reading *The Moor's Last Sigh*. I'd give anything to be able to tell Rushdie how wonderful it is! The way he uses English is marvellous, and the result is a completely "Indian" narrative. D H Lawrence ... I like to read science fiction or intelligence records at libraries. I remember coming across a list of local goondas in one of those records. Each name conjured up a colourful personality in my mind – it was fascinating!

I also keep track of new writing in Hindi. As for poetry, I like to read aloud the poems of Pash or "The Song of Songs" from the *Bible*. When I first read a poem I just let myself feel it. Then I try to intellectually "know" it in the second reading. This makes poetry an exciting and distinct kind of writing for me.

TB: *Weren't you also writing poetry once?*

KS: Yes, but I discovered my temperament was too prosaic for good poetry.

JS: *What do you feel about the kind of critical response your work gets?*

KS: It can be strange at times. For instance, *Ai Ladki* has been interpreted as a work obsessed with a "hunger for men!" See, once you become established as a writer, you keep getting a uniform, predictable kind of response. But then, I don't know. I might come out with a bad book tomorrow which might evoke very negative reactions. So there's no way I can take critics for granted.

READING OTHER WRITERS HAS HELPED ME KNOW MY LIMITATIONS, TO RECOGNIZE WORK THAT IS NOT GOOD ENOUGH.

JS: *What about your publishers?*

KS: I have had a long association with Rajkamal. My relationship with them, and with Sheela Sandhu in particular, has been wonderful. I don't reduce it to mere "public relations." You have to be friendly but matter-of-fact with your publishers and you can't take them for granted. You should not expect them to publish everything you write. I never took Rajkamal for granted even though they are my sole publishers.

***JS:** And your editors?*

KS: I do get a little anxious when I meet my editors. I respect them but don't like to get friendly with them. I remember when "Sikka Badal Gaya" was published in Vatsayayan's *Prateek*. I got my copy of the magazine from him, but I put it away. But after dinner that night, I took it out to see how many editorial changes had been made. There were none.

***TB:** So it is a delicate relationship?*

KS: Yes! Editors have the power to chop bits from your work. I too get that kind of a kick when I get rid of lines , a redundant passage. Or when I am writing as Hashmat. Then I assume some extra power and a masculine form – my stance changes, my language is different, I take on a new personality. In fact my handwriting too changes!

***TB:** Krishnaji, who is Hashmat?*

KS: My spiritual double – if at all I have any spirituality.

***TB:** And when did you meet Hashmat?*

KS: *Ek Daawat Mein Shirkat*, the first piece by Hashmat, was written after a party. There were quite a few people there – many of them writers. I felt I was different from them. Most of them seemed to be asking the same old questions in the same tired idiom. By the time I got home something had been transformed within me. That night there was a new presence at my table and I found myself writing with a sort of masculine hand. I felt threatened – What was I doing? Was I crossing over for good to something new and different? Later I realized Hashmat was there to stay. Fortunately Sobti and Hashmat decided to respect each other, to coexist peacefully.

***TB:** Does the name mean anything special?*

KS: It first came to me as a sound. In Urdu it refers to a person who is her/his own boss. Interestingly, the same word can be used for both "servant" and "master." You know, the first piece really shocked me – Hashmat's language was nothing like mine. I guess I had absorbed it somewhere.

***JS:** Absorbed it?*

KS: Yes, like I am absorbing yours now. As I talk to you, my language is drawing into it the magic of a "younger" language.

***TB:** Your pieces as Hashmat are normally described as pen-portraits. Is that what they are meant to be?*

KS: I didn't bother to correct my publishers when they were classified as that. But they are much more than pen-portraits of the people I know and they are not fiction either. See, a writer lives a literature apart from the one she creates – a large area where we writers interact with other writers, read each other's works. Hashmat was an attempt to find meaning in this area. I did take a few liberties with my contemporaries – as Hashmat I almost felt that I was an author! What I wanted to do was to preserve that sense of all of us being a community of writers.

YOU KNOW, THE FIRST PIECE [BY HASHMAT] REALLY SHOCKED ME – HASHMAT'S LANGUAGE WAS NOTHING LIKE MINE.

***TB:** Quite a few Hashmat encounters happen in some restaurant or the other. The reader gets the feeling that Hindi writers regularly congregate in coffee houses. Is that so?*

KS: Oh, I could write a whole book about the restaurant culture of the 60s and 70s. I remember when I was living in Riviera Apartments near Delhi University, I would often be at the University Coffee House. Jeet Oberoi once said about me, "Her flat was an open house ... she is the only Hindi writer who can afford to live on her royalties." I was delighted by what he had said, but it's hardly true. The Hindi publishing structure is just not geared for the effective marketing of books. In the Third World, no one can survive on royalties.

TB: *Did you face any problems in being accepted into this community of writers? One gets the impression that the Hindi literary world is fairly "male" in its orientation?*

KS: It is! Our Hindi world has a peculiar relationship with its women. They want to feel free with you ... make you wait on them. This used to irritate me a great deal. Now I know that they just can't treat you as an equal – either they are patronizing or they put you on a pedestal. Though I must confess they did not treat me quite like that. Probably because I was too much of an individual. I didn't have the inhibitions that most women feel in a predominantly male setup. Anyway, I've enjoyed myself, I've had the privilege of knowing three generations of writers – people like Bhagwati Charan Verma, Yashpaal, Jainendra, Vatsyayan.

JS: *And what are these inhibitions that most women have?*

KS: Men do not allow women to share the world they inhabit, and the region outside the house becomes almost exclusively male. Which is why I have chosen to live alone and to inhabit both worlds – the one within the walls of my house and the other one beyond it.

Personally, I feel that having a family of one's own can be a handicap for a writer. Women writers are so often asked, "Doesn't your husband object to your writing?" This question always makes me cringe, but I can't deny that there is the possibility of a husband objecting. And there is so much "noise" in a family situation. Just the presence of some people can be a deterrent to your work. A married existence in a family is anti-writing.

JS: *Did you have to struggle to make your present lifestyle possible?*

KS: No, not really. I have always had a very exact notion of "freedom." My parents, my family knew that I would go ahead and do just what I wanted. I like living on my own.

JS: *I am sure you are constantly asked to speak as a woman writer? How do you feel about this?*

KS: A while ago I was invited to inaugurate a seminar on "The Craft of Women" in Bhopal. As a woman, I don't really have the proper credentials. I haven't converted any house into a "home," I have not "made" any babies.

I constantly react to things ... protest is a way of life for me. At Bhopal, I noticed that apart from the women present, no one else was interested in talking of women's writing. I told those men, "Listen! All of you have been at writing for years and years. But for women it is a new art, their work has a freshness which stems from protest. They are striking at your well-entrenched patriarchal models, and you are worried. You would still like to think of women in terms of princess, mother, whore and wife."

When men feel threatened, they launch into their scriptural journeys. At this seminar, they decided to find the right word for "love" based on their readings of ancient texts. I wanted to hit out hard at them, and without wasting too many words. I wanted to tell them, "So many things have happened – changes that you just don't seem to be aware of. Look, one word for love could describe what you feel in your heart. Or it may be about sleeping together. Or about living with someone and making babies, or even deciding that you will not make babies and you will have separate bank accounts. It may also mean looking at the world with a shared vision. There are so many shades, but some people like you are interested only in defining unchanging universal categories. Is it any wonder then that to examine the most important happening of the twentieth century you continue to refer to ancient texts like Manu's! This intellectual brahminism has to go."

> THE HINDI PUBLISHING STRUCTURE IS JUST NOT GEARED FOR THE EFFECTIVE MARKETING OF BOOKS.

***TB:** What is your perception of the kind of status of Hindi and*

Hindi literature are being given?

KS: Once, at some party, Mulk Raj Anand challenged me, saying, "Can you give me the names of four good novels after Premchand's?" I said, "Shall we talk about the weather?" He persisted, "I'm asking for four names." So I said, "Sahab, I like your outfit, I'm impressed by your tight pants ..." He says, "No, please ..." and then I asked him, "When did you read your last Hindi novel?" His answer was, "Twenty-five years ago." I told him then, "Don't slight my language. I'll fight to the end ... and don't compel me to say anything about Indian writing in English."

My attitude is that when my primary reader is not the English-speaking person, then why should I keep such a reader in mind while writing? I know that when Adil Jussawala wanted *Mitro Marjani* for the book he was editing – *The Penguin Anthology of Indian Writing* – and it was not used ultimately as a translator was not forthcoming, I was not too bothered. I cannot make it my priority to consider how people would read it in English. I regard it as being complete in its present form. Anyway, Hindi is being enriched, it is acquiring words from various dialects, languages and disciplines. It is now capable of describing anything. Look at English, look at the kinds of words and shades of meanings it has developed over the centuries.

***TB:** What do you think of the new generation of writers in Hindi?*

KS: Some of them are very good. But they seem to be too aware of the political apparatus. They should protect democratic values. After all, we don't want an ideological dictatorship, do we? We need to cultivate a "citizen culture."

***JS:** What do you plan to write next?*

KS: My first novel is back on my table. I'm working on the second part of the *Zindaginama* trilogy. But let me tell you something about me. I take things easy. Once in a while when I decide to act, it is like an army drill. I am on the job. In my shoes that are not big. Not small. But just the right size for me stand erect!

***TB:** Do you watch TV or films?*

KS: The first film I saw was *Mahatma* – sometime in the 30s. I have seen a lot of films – Hindi and English – but very few films engage you intellectually. I also watch a lot of television. It's interesting to see the new "working class" culture. Something like *Mere Message Mere Geet*. It's amazing, the number of people who send requests for such programmes.

JS: *Is there something really special that you'd like to write some day?*

KS: Something based on the changing quality of the lives of old people, and how they are creating lifestyles for themselves now. The institution of the family has evolved quite a bit. It should change some more so that old people can be part of the same landscape as the rest of the family, their dignity preserved.

AI LADKI!

translated by
Anjali Singh &
Tarun Bhartiya

Ladki, your mother looked beautiful as a bride. People adored her ... But how Time turns against you! In one phase of your life you climb up the stairs. In the next, you go back – down those same stairs. No one can glow for ever.

— Ammu, what did you think of your *new* family?

— Don't you think too highly of *your* family! By the time I arrived, their prestige was on the decline. They were courteous and polite, yet proud and arrogant, and traces of their glory, though faded, still remained. They had their share of the good and the bad times – it poured in some places, others were absolutely dry!

— Ammu, tell me about Pitaji.
— Hanh, once the rot sets in, it eats up the insides of the family. There is no stopping it ... Your father, he was a quiet man. Very solemn. I was a little hard. But I was eager to learn. And I did. I learnt a lot from him.
Then, erupting suddenly –
— Ladki, why are you making me chew on the same old cud all the while? Who are you trying to entertain – me or yourself? Age strips away all your dignity. It is a monster that devours you. I'm a burden on everyone now. Why, why did I have to live this long?

My daughter's son died at twenty-seven ... What physique, what looks, what a personality he had! It was so unfair. But there could be no plea, nor protest – not here, not there. It was murder, not a death ... Ladki, show me his photograph. He is right in front of my eyes ... We needed you, beta. Why were you snatched away? Wasn't it the day of the engagement? Your fiancée was left waiting, still in her finery. The ring never touched her finger ... Ladki, we are just puppets in His hands.

But, do you know what my eldest grandson did then? He put himself to the test and walked the same path. He brought his brother's betrothed home, made her the bahu of the family ... We tried everything, but Chitra beti, Time was never on your side. It was all over, in a year ...

❦

— Susan, can you put some drops into my eyes. These eyes are old now.
— Ammiji, Horlicks, cocoa or tea?
— Whatever you want to give me! Has Didi left the room?
— She is lying down for a while.
— Cover me with the blanket, Susan.
— The blanket? It's hot, Ammiji!

This extract is the last part (pp 67-119) of Krishna Sobti's novella *Ai Ladki,* Rajkamal Prakashan, 1991. This piece has been translated exclusively for Katha.

— Do as you are told! You know nothing about the taal of this raag. All you do is make entries into that timetable of yours. Gave her medicine. Changed the dressing. Gave an injection. Checked her temperature. Called the doctor. Made her turn sides once ...

Why are you laughing? Your records will go into the wastepaper basket. That's where all records go!

— Ammiji, I'll get some Horlicks for you.

— No! No! Do something about my head instead – it's spinning.

As Susan oils her hair, Ammi dozes off.

❦

After a nap –

— Hasn't Didi got up yet? Is she still sleeping?

— Ji.

— My nails are bothering me. Here, clip them.

— Ammiji, I'd trimmed them just yesterday.

— Maybe, but can't you do it again for my peace of mind?

❦

— Susan, are your brothers married and settled?

— Ji Ammiji, both of them.

— Your parents – do you send them any money?

— Ji.

— You will have to find a husband on your own, won't you? Do you have anyone in mind?

— No Ammiji, not yet. I want to train as a nurse first.

— Good decision! Stick to it, Susan. Don't give it up halfway through. But you must be having a friend or two ...

Susan smiles.

— I hope you don't spend too much money on him.

Susan laughs now.

— No, Ammiji!

— Take my advice – don't pay for everything, but don't let him bear all the expenses either. Keep it at fifty-fifty. Or you'll find yourself being completely swallowed one day. Do you understand what I am saying?

— Ji, Ammiji.

— Susan, when you get married, make sure you don't turn into anyone's puppet. Try to be strong.

That's the door bell. See who is at the door ... Who's it?

— No one, Ammiji.

— Check again. Shobharam should be coming now.

— Ammiji, he's in the kitchen already. He came a long while ago.

— Ask him if the kheer is ready. This morning he said he would make some.

— Ammiji, pranam!

— May you live long!

— Won't you taste it, Ammiji?

— A little. Only two spoonfuls.

— Here! It has pistas too.

— You know that my teeth are still very strong, don't you?.

— Of course they are! Ammiji, shall we make puas too in the evening?

— No, no. We can't have too much rich food. I'll tell you some day what food should be served with what. The challans I have got for that!

The woman, drawing closer –

— What's this about challans, Ammu?

— Shobharam, the kheer's turned out well. Keep making nice things for me to eat. Halwa-puri-kheer-pua-pakora. But I'm entrusting you with another job too – you will have to take Amma there ...

The woman, softly –

— Ammu, what was that challan incident?

— Nothing much. The usual bickering over what was to be cooked! If it ever turned into a big argument, I would put the tea tray in front

of your father, saying, The tea's waiting for you, why don't you pay some attention to it now? He was a connoisseur of tea. It could make him forget everything else.
— Ammu, did you really have so many fights?
— Probably. I can't remember now. Why are you trying to needle me? Do you have to know all that?
— What's wrong if I do!
— Ladki, everyone's journey through life is a series of offensives and counter-offensives. But the game played within the walls of the home is an unequal contest. The master of the house earns and provides for everybody, thus securing and consolidating his power. The mother of his children finds herself mortgaged to his masterful generosity.
— Ammu!
— A woman, after her marriage, is made to row the family shikara. You have seen the boats and shikaras floating on lakes, haven't you? While she works the oar, the rest of the family enjoys itself. She keeps at it all her life. Things can change for her only if she starts earning too. Just think – men get paid for their efforts, what does a woman get for slogging day and night? It's like bonded labour! She's trapped in mushy maternal sentiments – ignorant, unaware. If she doesn't question her own lot, who will?
— You're so progressive, Ammu!
— Shut up, Ladki! You pounce and hold on to whatever I say. Why? I can see through your charade – you are planning to make *my* experiences *your* wisdom.
Looking towards the window –
— Change these heavy curtains, I want to get some fresh air. Ladki, let me be quiet for sometime. I feel something unraveling within me.
She shuts her eyes. After some time she opens them and sees the woman there –
— You're still here! Tell me, what are you doing with your life? Do you have anything to show for yourself, anything at all that you

have earned in this life? What is your worth? And *you* are auditing my accounts!

The woman gets up –

— I'm going.

— No! Stay. Stay with me for a while. I'll talk of things that might interest you. I have very little time left.

Ladki, where are you – at which turning in life?Are you in a queue with other people? All right, let me tell you. You are standing at the doorsteps of your siblings.

— Ammu, not again ...

— Don't interrupt! Hear me out. I have a happy family – sons, daughters, grandchildren. Yet I am all alone. But you, you are not part of this timeless family saga. You may not have crossed the threshold of wordly affairs, but you are a person in your own right. Ladki, it's supreme, it's sublime to be complete in yourself. If you had ever pulled the family cart you would know that all the glory of a housewife is a farce. A woman is a queen just in name, she is either a wife, a daughter-in-law, a mother, or a grandmother. With the same old preoccupation with food, clothes, and jewellery. Wiped of all individuality, she is cast in a mould and put in her place.

The woman laughs –

— Ammu, you're quite something!

— If you enquire carefully, any question can be answered.

— Susan, get some juice for Ammu. And for me too. I want mine chilled.

— Quite appropriate – the juice of fruits to flow through our lonely lives.

— That was nice, Susan. It quenched my thirst. You have no idea, Ladki, of the qualities a woman in a family must cultivate, the restraint she has to practice. You are a free person. You can do what you want. But remember, you need to be free from yourself too. Have you been able to do that? I am not talking about impulses.

Have you been able to follow your dreams?
— Ammu, what should I say?
There is silence in the room for a long while.
— I took good care of this family, but I never did anything for myself. I regret it now.
The woman is surprised –
— What, Ammu? What did you want to do?
— I wanted to climb mountains, conquer peaks. But it did not fit in with the household routine. Who could have I talked to about it? Your father? Impossible. He had a hard time just taking care of the family problems. Besides, he was a stickler for things happpening on time. I remained nothing but a timepiece.
The woman looks out of the window. Susan starts folding clothes.
Ammu, irritated –
— Why are you folding them? There is no newborn in the house, only a hag on her way out. And piles of her old clothes ...
The daughter gets up to play a record.
Ammu listens to it for a while. Then, in a sharp, agitated tone –
Shut it off! This noise is not good for me. Try to understand. The streams within me are dry, so these tunes rattle my insides. Why do I see black threads in front of my eyes? Ask someone!

❦

As Susan covers Ammi with a blanket, she throws it off and sits up.
— Why are you people troubling me? Pull the curtains. Let in some fresh air. Quick! I am suffocating. Why are you quiet? Listen to me carefully. I am not asking for the sky, only what is rightfully mine. Let me breathe fresh air.
Susan pulls the curtains aside –
— Ammiji, the glare will bother you.
— This is a cave. Why have you shut me in? Open the door. Who bolted it? Call whoever is playing this game with me. And please call my daughter. I want to go to the balcony. I won't stay here another minute.

— Susan, give Ammi some Electral. I'll make some place for her in the balcony.
— Don't ignore my wishes, Ladki. I want to sit in a chair. I will not lie down. I want to sit. Today, you must decide in my favour, Ladki.
— Ammi, your sores will get worse if you move.
— I don't need your sympathies, neither do my sores. Do as I tell you!

❦

Susan pulls an armchair into the balcony and places a cushion and a sheet on it. They lift Ammi and bring her to the balcony.
Ammi, excited –
—What season is this? Everything is so still! Not a leaf moves. What month is it?
The woman ignores her. She stands quietly, her hands on the railing.
— I asked you something. Reply! Such disobedience is not proper.
— Ammi, it is the third week of May. A storm is on its way. Look up. The sky bears a dusty pall. It looks strange, as if drained of its strength by its children.
— Ladki, the sky, too, seems to have aged.
Ammi lifts her head to look at the electricity poles. Then she looks down at the trees –
— These neem trees outlast human plants.
— Ammu, they have grown well. The one outside your room is really big.
— This time of the year, the neem is fragrant. It arouses the women of the earth.
— What then, Ammu?
— Well, they go to people who can satisfy their needs. All these problems come with one's body!

Ladki, the moisture on the shores has dried and this fish is struggling again. I am very thirsty. Get me some soda with icecream. And put another chair here. My son is coming straight from his office.

The woman is quiet. Ammu, to herself –

— A true woman must be able to subdue her man's mother.

— Ammu, have you had do that?

— I must have. Everybody does.

— Is it necessary?

— You could say that! A woman stamps her ownership over the man's body and soul. She has to, otherwise her well-being is in jeopardy. *(laughs)* Everyone is different. Some suspect, others believe. These men understand everything. The secret of keeping a family together is the same – give and receive. If one gives, one must receive.

Susan feeds Ammu icecream with a spoon.

— May you live long. I'm at peace now.

Ammu is taken back to the room –

— This icecream reminded me of the pista kulfi I ate at Chandpal Ghat.

— Was it special, Ammu?

— Yes, the place and the time. It mesmerized everyone who passed by.

Ships in anchor. Blaring horns. Lights shimmering across the water. Waves battling each other. Boats bobbing in the sea. A mela on the banks. The sky, stretched over the living world like a canopy, studded with twinkling stars and adorned by a beautiful moon. Ladki, in this world there are spectacular vistas of earth and water. Who would ever want to leave this and go? But, everyone must leave sometime.

When I went to Calcutta I roamed around a lot! Once my eldest daughter took me and her granddaughter there. Three generations together – my daughter, my grandson's daughter and I. Children rejuvenate you. At first they make you feel your age, but then you forget that as you get involved. That evening, your sister behaved as if she was the older one and I, her mother, was younger than her. Her naughty granddaughter was convinced that her father's grandmother was both old and young at the same time. She kept offering,

"Nani Ma, have another ice cream. We will share it, half and half ..."

When time and place come together, the essence of a family blooms fragrantly. Wait Ladki, I can see something through my mind's peephole ...

— What is it, Ammu?

Ammu laughs, toothlessly –

— A swift, strong horse. You never learnt to ride, did you? For the sake of your health and for the horse, you should have taken it out for rides

Ladki, Those who move with the times are favoured by Time. The hand that acquires is the same hand that gives freely.

The woman gazes into the distance, as if she can see through the walls, and then closes her eyes.

— If you are bored, go for a walk.

The woman steps out of the room and returns in a fresh set of clothes.

— Ammu, I am going out for coffee. Do you want me to get something for you? Pineapples, pastries?

— I'd like that. Take your own time, don't worry about me. You will find me here. I'll still be around.

If you go for a haircut, tell them I need one too. My hair feels too heavy, it's almost unmanageable.

— Susan, keep everything ready – the shampoo, the oil, the towel. These people have very little time to spare. If they come here before I return, get Ammu's hair cut.

Is that okay, Ammu?

— Yes.

❦

— That's my daughter! Without her the room seems so pale and colourless.

— Ammiji, Didi loves you a lot.

— She loves *and* understands her mother. There is a difference. To love is not the same as to know. She is always eager to help others.

Susan, Didi looks distracted. I wonder what it is?
— Nothing, Ammiji. She gets tired.
— Will you be able to look after her when I am gone? She needs a lot of rest. She gets too involved with her work, she is not scared of working hard. It would be nice if you continued to live here. She may seem a little stern but she keeps everyone's concerns in mind.

Do me a favour, Susan. Go out and look at the colour of the sky. Is there a chance of rain? If it rains, I will bathe in the open! My back is in a mess. Medicines, bandages ... and everything else.
— The sores are healing, Ammiji.
— Don't try to fool me! You can see as you clean them, I cannot. But I know because I have to bear the pain.
Laughs–
— Susan, people can't see their backs with their eyes. I know how bad it is only because I endure it.
— Anyway, tell me, have you ever got wet in the rain? No hot or cold shower can come close to the experience. I have bathed in lakes, ponds, rivers, even the sea. My eldest daughter took me to Puri once.
— Ammiji, you keep thinking of Badi Didi.
— Why shouldn't I? She's my first daughter after all. There were more boys in my in-laws' family. So there was a lot of celebration when she was born.
— And Ammiji, this Didi?
— She is a sensible sort but once she makes up her mind, nothing can move her. Parents pass their traits on to their children. The mould and the clay decide a child's character.
Ammu strains to listen –
— Someone is at the door. Must be my son.
— Ammiji, there is nobody there.
— Check again ... It may be Prabha, my eldest granddaughter. She is also like her father – devoted to her work. You've met young Meera, haven't you? She is so charming! She keeps coming here to meet her nani. Come now, wipe my face with a cold towel. And my neck

too. Susan, my neck cannot bear the weight of this hair any more.

❦

The woman returns –

— Nice haircut, Ammu. You look better.

— What do you think – my face started to glow as soon as you left?

— No Ammu, short hair suits you.

— I wonder why I did not think of it earlier. I feel light now!

When I was young, I used to feel that all the restrictions of the world were twisted into a bride's plait. A few days after I came to your father's house, he said – Doesn't this long plait bother you? You must be feeling all tied up. So I told him – I would like to keep a tiny one, but I am not supposed to. So he explained to me – There's no custom here that cannot be changed. Do what is comfortable and convenient for you.

— Ammu, and how did it feel to hear that?

— Great! I realized that we would get along well. Your father was extremely gentle and careful. No unnecessary restrictions were imposed on me. But we were not allowed to jeopardize the family honour. That was a strict rule.

— Ammu, that is bigotry.

— No, it is discipline! Your grandfather's sense of propriety was remarkable. Father and son were equals – they wielded almost the same influence inn the house. I learnt the meaning of equality here since no distinction was made between boys and girls. Listen carefully, Ladki, you belong to a family that does not believe in discrimination.

— And Ammu, what about Nana – your father?

— Let that be! It isn't fair to compare.

— Ammu, tell me, please.

— Ladki, there was no dearth of love and affection at your nana's place. Food, clothes, toys, they were all in abundance. But there was a clear, deep line separating boys and girls.

When your nana was in the terminal stage of his illness, though all his daughters were present, he would keep asking for his son. I felt dejected. And I could never accept his overwhelming love for his son at his deathbed. Even your mind grows old, along with your body ... What was I saying? Ah yes, my brother was sent to college and we sisters were sent to pandits and maulvis. Think about it. If I had got the same kind of education as my brother did, I could have been anything! My children would have been different! The truth is that girls are trained to serve – Your brother is studying, give him milk. He is sleeping, go cover him with a blanket. He is hungry, serve him food quickly. He has finished eating, now you can eat.

Ammu is quiet for some time.

Susan bends low and asks –

— What's the matter, Ammiji?

Ammu, sounding scared –

— My eyes are burning! I can feel the smoke. What's going on?

The woman rushes to the kitchen, comes back immediately.

— There seems to be a coat of fog over my eyes! I can't see anything clearly.

— Ammu, this will make you feel better.

— What are you putting on my eyes?

— Cream, Ammu.

— Come here, Ladki. Tell your mother the truth. You have soothed my eyes, but have you ever felt such a soothing sensation yourself?

— No, Ammu.

The room is quiet for a long time.

Suddenly, Ammu, quite unaware of herself –

— When is it going to be the full moon? How old is the new moon? Tell me. I am asking you.

The woman replies, sternly–

— I don't keep track of days.

— No wonder you are carrying that burden on your shoulder. Throw it! Fling it far! Learn even now before it is too late. Ladki, don't ignore Time. It's like water on a slope.

The woman leaves the room. Susan gives Ammi some glucose. Ammi, talking to herself –
— When I was carrying this girl, a strange loneliness had enveloped me. I wanted desperately to be alone, wandering through small lanes. It felt as though a pine tree was growing inside me. That is what happened. A tree. It has grown. It's moving in the wind – just swaying. Nothing stands in front of her. Don't ever think that she is cold. She has fire in her eyes. She restrains herself, I don't know how.

❦

— Susan, the bell! It must be Beeba–Bobby, my son's children.
— Ammiji, they have gone to their nani's house.
— Yes, to console her. Poor woman, she must be upset because I am dying. Susan, you've met Bobby, haven't you? He is just like his grandfather. Those manners, the gestures, his eating habits ...
Ammi drifts off to sleep.
After a while she gets up, looks around as if trying to identify the room. Spotting the woman near her bed, she shouts –
— Who are you? You walk in and storm out whenever you please. I know that face. It is your father's. But Ladki, your father had no pride. Your head is packed with it. That is why you have not shared anything with anyone ever.
The woman tip-toes out of the room.

❦

— Susan, my granddaughter's piggybank is in the almirah, don't misplace it. There are seelam threads on the clothesrack. They are for my granddaughter's doll. I'll give the doll hair and plait that hair.

Why are the windows banging? What is that flying in the air? Oh, it's my odhni! Hold it or it will blow away in the storm.
Susan rushes to call Didi. Both bend to look at her –
— She's in deep sleep. Susan, rest for a while. I'm here.

Ammu wakes up. In sharp tones —
— Susan, where are you? Change the bedsheets. They are wet.
Susan wipes Amma clean and replaces the covers.

❦

Ammu wakes up suddenly, after a long, deep sleep.
— Can you hear the sounds of the train? It hasn't reached the station yet, but the sound of the engine rushes here to settle inside me.
The woman runs a hand over her mother's hair.
— Just before he left us, your father would spring up and sit on the bed each time he heard the sound of the four-o-clock morning train. I would watch him silently. Never questioned him about it. What was left to ask, anyway?

One night, he woke to a shuddering sound – just like the one I heard a little while ago – and, propping his elbow at the head of the bed, leant over me. He said, Did you hear that sound? It fills me with great sorrow.

I was silent. What could I say! When your time is about to run out, all kinds of strange things begin to strike at your heart. All the happiness of days past travels backwards and your soul moves towards the infinite – they return where they had come from!
The woman touches her mother's wrist, pretending to straighten the sheet that covers her.
Ammu, sweetly —
— This relic's still holding on. Rest for a while.
The woman, trying to hide her embarrassment —
— Ammu, I'm going to make coffee for myself. Should I get some for you too?
— Na. If you really want to make me eat, get me some fresh fruit.
— Aam or aalubukhara?
— Aam ... the name suits the fruit.
— Ladki, your sister knows how to cut fruits — she slices the aam into two, makes holes into with a fork and then covers it with cream.

Both your eyes and your mind get their fill of its taste.
— You must have taught her how to do it.
— No, such sophistication belongs to this house. Not to mine.
The woman, laughing —
— Ammi, how did you suddenly get into this discussion of *your* house and *my* house?
— Why should it surprise you? When a woman sends out roots in a new place, she pushes the memories of her home into the backyard of her heart. Look at your mother — she is thinking of her people now, at the fag end of her life!
— Ammu, the occasions for conflict are no longer past. Why did these thoughts of a struggle between the two houses rise in your mind suddenly?
— Innocent thoughts ... I never had the time to think of this, but today I can see both houses clearly — each distinct from the other, each in its own special colours.
— Ammu, so who is the winner?
— Don't think too well of yourself, Ladki! My family wasn't any less than this one!
— And you are a true descendant of theirs! Didn't you have complete sway over this house?
— No, ri. No outsider can ever count with your khandaan. This family can swallow all competition.
— Don't say that! You have always run this household.
— I must say that your khandaan is a very colourless one. God knows what they think, or what they see. They are too wrapped up in themselves.
— Amma, do we all seem the same to you?
— Of course. That's the way you are, and always were. My people were as good, but they didn't put themselves on pedestals. Here, everyone bears a little inscription.
— Ammu, why are you saying such things now?
— Let me! I won't come back. This is my last chance to settle all accounts. When a woman enters a new household, she is mixed

and churned properly. It's almost like an earthquake. But she accepts it, because she has to.

— Ammu, how would you feel if you had to come into this family again?

Ammu stares at the woman with anger, then begins to laugh —

— You, old woman of this khandaan ... if I were asked before being sent down next time, I would choose this house. The relics of your ancestors are still preserved here, the family I made is here, so why should I go looking for another door?

The woman kisses her mother's forehead, all the while trying to keep her emotions in check.

— Ages – I've been alive for ages! I keep thinking these days, why couldn't I do something worthwhile if I had to live so long. It's a big, wide world. I could have at least tried to see all of it. But I spent a lifetime caught in the warp and the weft of this household.

— Ammu, you've done so much. You've created a whole family.

— Don't make it into more than what it is, Ladki! I might have given birth to all of you, but I am different from you. I am I. I am not you, and you are not me.

— Listen to me, please ...

Amma explodes —

— All your respect is of no use to me. Listen Ladki, a child gobbles up all her mother's time.

— Ammu, there must be someone who gives you a little happiness, or a sense of satisfaction.

— That's not what I am talking about. A mother gives birth to children, raises them. And then she is sacrificed. Her family divides her into little bits and spreads them around. Why? Because if she were whole she might rise and ask for her rights. Mothers are kept only as maids or breeding cows. So that she can slave. And give comfort to others. That's all she is supposed to do. Doesn't matter what she considers herself to be, for her children she is only the housekeeper.

Susan switches on the soft bedside light and Ammu closes her eyes.

At midnight, waking up —

— Susan, tell me the exact time. Is it still night or is dawn about to break?

— It's 2 pm, Ammiji.

— The night seems to be crawling. Hanh, do something about my throat. God knows what is wrong with it. I have nothing to do so I lie in bed and talk – flitting over the years gone by, rushing like a hurtling train.

Susan gives her some water.

— There must be some sugar cubes lying around.

— I'll just get some, Ammiji.

— This corporeal machinery was made to last a hundred years. It was running smoothly enough. But for that fractured bone, I would still be fine.

— What is this, Ammiji? You've removed the dressing again.

— Yes, I did. I've only freed what was bound.

Susan turns Ammi over to clean the wound and dress it again.

— Susan, listen to me. Leave it open now.

— Ammiji, it might begin to fester.

— Why are you arguing? Don't I know what this pain is like? I am not wearing a suit of armour. I'm sleeping on a bed of arrows.

❦

— Susan, has it gone?

— Do you mean the train, Ammiji? Which one?

— You are not doing your duty, you've become careless. You've been here for months and you still don't know when it comes or goes.

— But the station is very far from here, Ammiji.

— I'm not talking of the station. The van first collects the empty milk bottle from the depot and then goes there again to deposit the full bottles.

Susan picks up the thermos.

— Ammiji, milk or Complan?

— Neither. Take me to Didi's room.
— Let me first ask Didi.
— Ask Didi? That room too is a part of my house. Don't make me feel like a handicapped person. Take me to the small room so that I can pay my respects to the deities. And then to Didi.
Susan picks up Ammi in her arms. The woman wakes up, hearing the footsteps –
— Susan, what is this? Ammu, why are you here at this hour?
— You haven't slept yet, Ladki. Is there any harm in my lying here and talking to you for a while.
— No, Ammu.
The woman puts a cushion on the diwan.
— Susan, carefully ... here. Are you comfortable, Ammu?
— Hanh.
Have you started writing something new?
— No, Ammu. It was an old half-done piece. I thought I should look at it again.
— Don't waste too much time on thought. Wrap up things. Time is fast running out. Yes, but remember never to underestimate your work. This too is creation, and not any less productive than other occupations. Life is made of a thousand streams and one never knows which direction a stream might choose to flow in.
Ammū, after a moment's pause –
— As I lay in my room I realized that you and I – mother and daughter – have grown apart, just as night and day move away from each other. I looked around. Saw that I was still in my room, still in this world. So I thought, Let me go and meet my daughter. So, here I am. Susan wasn't willing but ...
Ammu smiles –
— To resolve and accomplish is the greatest blessing of all. Hanh, don't miss me too much. Only as much as you need to. Take some time off to travel. You look tired.
A long silence.
— Will you keep Susan on?
— No, Ammi.

— And the cook?
— He'll go too.
— Can't you keep at least one of them?
— It'll make things more difficult.
— If there are enough vegetables, milk, curds, paneer in the fridge, it won't take much effort. Cooking and serving keep one happy.
— Ji.
— You must think of your future too. Everything has been held up. How will you manage alone?
— Somehow, Ammu.
Ammu, a little unsure –
— You can do anything you set your mind to. Nothing is too big or too small to be tackled.
The woman's gaze is fixed on her mother.
— Don't do anything that goes against your grain.
— Ammu, is there anything signficant that you want to tell me about?
— No one owes me any land or gold or cattle. All I have is plain advice. Ladki, a daughter can't be the head of the family. Your brother will take on that mantle, in accordance with the scriptures. And the bahu takes charge of the rest.

❦

— The keys of the locker are in my almirah. In a round box on the upper shelf. Once we had kilos of gold, Ladki. You will find only a few grams now. We used it whenever the need arose ... but you know all that ....

I have written out the papers. Show them to your brothers and sisters. Bahu has a locker of her own and her valuables are with her. If her mother-in-law's gift doesn't reach her on her vidaai, I'll ask Goddess Bhawani for forgiveness. Families own much less than they appear to. Who owns what, why and how much – it's all too mixed up. But don't get into any arguments. The others are complete and you are not a part of their circle. Ladki, you will be alone.

The woman lights a cigarette. Laughing –
— Ammu, you can have a puff if you like.
— You will have to prop me up with pillows.
— That's hardly a problem. Here.
Ammu, visibly enjoying herself –
— Ladki, when your inner voice speaks, you must listen to it. Wasn't it nice that I came here?Or I would have still been wandering in the darkness.
The woman, in a light tone –
— Ammu, Susan wasn't really wrong. It must have been difficult to lift you from the bed.
— It was just from one room to another. I can't come from the other world to meet you, can I?
— Ji Ammu.
— Some moments hang in the smoke. Can I ask you something?
— Yes, Ammi.
— This flat, who owns it?
— You, in my absence.
— I give it to you then!
Both burst out laughing. Ammu, in a changed, somewhat strange voice –
— We shouldn't be laughing really. It's quite sad.
— Ammu it's not important enough to make us turn our laughter into tears.
— But it's not so unimportant either that you should not think about it. I see myself in you. But you have inherited your temperament from your father's family.
— Is that a blessing or a fault?
— Not quite a blessing, but not completely a fault either.
— So you've stamped it with your brand of doubt. Ammu, this doesn't prove anything.
— Ladki, what will you prove in your solitary journey. A life of companionship washes a few traces away, and leaves behind a few. But in solitude, there's nothing to wash away or leave behind. Are you listening?

— Yes, Ammu.
— Ladki, there is a small circle of life within the bounds of a family. That's where a woman derives meaning for herself and others. As a mother, she experiences eternity. Since you don't have a family of your own, you live within yourself.
— And others, Ammu?
— They take care of their pigeon-holes! Whatever you have done for this family, Ladki, cannot be summed up by a mathematical formula - only by a mother's blessings.
Susan, peeps into the room to say -
— Should we take Ammiji to the other room now?
— Let her lie here for a while. Hanh, but get some cold water, ice, slices of lemon and two glasses. Then rest. I will call you if we need you.
Susan brings a tray and keeps it on the table.
— Ladki, your room looks nice and full.
— That's because you are here, Ammu.
The woman squeezes some lemon, adds ice and fills up the glasses. Ammi's eyes are fixed on her. She helps her mother sit up, against a few cushions.
— Ammu, will you be able to hold the glass?
— Yes.
— Here Ammu, cheers!
Ammu nods. A few sips later -
— Ladki, we will surely meet sometime, somewhere again and we'll recognize each other. It's a big world but it's unlikely that we will be mistaken. A mother and her daughter will always remain that. Till the end of the world.
The woman holds back her tears and looks at her mother. The she stares at the liquid in her glass for a long while. Raising the glass, she takes a deep gulp.

The next day. Ammi is quiet - a silence induced by some great sorrow. She removes her bangle and pushes them under the pillow. Throws the sheet in a heap on to the floor. Pulls out the pillow from under her head. The cushion is flung to the door. She turns her head from one side to the other in a desperate attempt to push away the sheet she is lying on.

Susan, as soon as she enters the room –

— Ammiji, what are you doing?

— Can't you see for yourself?

— But this is not the way to ...

— It is – when you really need to!

— Let me change the sheets, Ammiji.

❦

Ammu is silently removing the dressing. She pulls it away little-by-little. The cotton, and the gauze land in the hand-basin. Susan fetches Didi, meanwhile. The woman walks up to her mother, and in gentle tones –

— Ammu, what is happenening here?

— Exactly what you see.

— The wound will start oozing pus if you remove things that way. Is it because you are feeling warm?

— No. I'm cold.

The woman switches off the room cooler. Ammi, in anger –

— Hot, cold, I don't care. Just throw everything out.

Ammu tries to take off the chain around her throat.

— Remove this. I don't want it. I don't want anything any more.

The woman, lovingly –

— Ammu, don't do this.

Ammu stares at the woman, her eyes wide open, unblinking.

— If there's anything Ammu that you would like, that you want ...

Ammu, angry –

— Quiet!

— What's bothering you? Tell me. Please.

Ammu looks at the door for a while. Then she gestures to the woman

to come closer, as if she wants to whisper into her ear –
— Just as I have removed the sheet from over my frame, remove my body from me. I can't bear this any longer.
The woman bends over her mother. Alert, but stunned.
— Don't keep any of my clothes in the house. Send them away , far away. Banish them from your sight.
In a flash, a slight awareness of her mother's interior landscape seems to strike the woman. Controlling her voice –
— Ammu, whatever you say will be done. But I insist on one thing – I will not give your clothes away. I will wear them. Even if you object. You heard that, didn't you?
The strain from Ammu's face drains into the pillow.

❦

Next morning. Ammu seems bright and watchful –
— Susan, you are walking rather slowly. Didn't you sleep well last night?
— I did, Ammiji.
— So was I pretending to sleep? Susan, you sleep when your patient sleeps, and when she wakes up, you get up too.
Susan laughs.
— Come here, Susan. I have something to tell you.
The certificate is ready. It's been signed too. Consider it done now. Take a peek at the sky. See, if there are any clouds about.
Susan, returning from the balcony –
— The sun is beating down and the sky is absolutely clear. Not a single cloud could I see!
— Get my things ready for a bath then. I won't let you sponge my body today. I'll go to the bathroom and have a proper shower.
— Ammiji, shouldn't I check with Doctor Sahab?
— No, he's only responsible for the medicine and treatment. His work is over now because he is not really my doctor. Susan, there's a doctor who is greater than all these doctors. A doctor, who at the assigned moment, claims a whole human being as his fee.

— I'll wake up Didi.
— Let her sleep. A big responsiblity is about to fall on her shoulders. She should get some rest now. Hanh, show me the soap you have been using on me.
— Ammiji, this one.
— This soap is for children. It doesn't dry the skin. Get a bar of soap from the box in my cabinet.
The woman is standing nearby, looking troubled.
— Ammu have breakfast before you bathe.
— As you wish! What am I getting for breakfast?
— Whatever you want. Mango juice, toast, eggs, parantha, curds, butter.
Ammu begins to laugh –
— Do you want me to increase my weight before you send me to the other world? It's not as if I will be made to work there. Ladki, it is only in this world that human beings have the power to improve things with their effort. In the other one, there are no houses with chulhas burning in each of them. Nor are there bodies with fire flickering within them. Who has ever seen Baikunth Dham? For living beings, all the dhams are here in this world.
Ammu is lost in the world of sleep. Suddenly, startled –
— What's wrong with you two? How can you lie there unconcerned? Get up and see what's bothering me.
The woman, bending over her mother –
— Ammu, what is it?
— Those crows are making such a din. Caw-caw-caw. I can't bear the sound of their restless movements. Chase them away. So far that I can't hear them any more.
The woman opens the window and pretends to shoo away the birds. Then she shuts it and turns to Ammu to reassure her –
— You can sleep now. They've flown away, Ammu.
— Who?
— The pigeons, Ammu.
— Only pigeons?

— Yes.
— There must be a cat outside, waiting to pounce on them.
— No, Ammu, there's nothing there.
— You don't know, Ladki. There's a lion sitting there. It'll devour them.

❦

Susan gives her water with a spoon.

❦

— Who's left the lamp under the tree? There's a strong wind blowing. The light will die.

I am being broken. There are cracks in my body. My limbs are all falling apart, one by one.

Whose is this shimmering blue face? Has he come to collect me?

Call my son, quick ... Come close to me, son ... see me off.

❦

— Susan, why have you kept the room so dark?
Don't remove the ladder from under my feet.
I will climb on my own.
You lazy thing, get my white shoes.
I have to go up to the Mashobara.
Ladki, ask your father to wait for me.
I am coming.

❦

— Why are we taking the road past the Kalibari?
Buffaloes and goats must be getting slaughtered there.
Shoo-shoo-go away ...
A bronze-coloured man-eater is chasing me.
Where should I go? She will impale me with her horns.

Reams of darkness unfold, one after the other.
Why are they shrouding me in their folds?
Don't touch my eyes.
Ladki, call your brother.
Call him quick!
Ask him to let my horse loose.
I'll ride it across the sea.

❦

The woman, touching her mother's hand gently –
— Ammi, take a dip in the sea ... Everything will be fine!

❦

A long breath, a shudder, and then all quiet in the room.

ZINDAGINAMA: SOME NOTES

translated by
Ashutosh Roy

The now is joy,
The past, spent,
is part of history and fixed in time.
Joy belongs to the moment,
to each passing minute.
The joy of the moment,
the yearning for life,
the celebration of being,
and a desire to inscribe them in pages
– *Zindaginama*

... To put *Zindaginama* down on paper was not enough. I had to live it, like a lifetime. Tend to it, like crops in a field. What happened was that I spotted a piece of fresh earth. I did have a right to it after all – partly because I wanted it. And also because it was my inheritance. So I staked my claim to it. Marked its boundaries. Levelled the land. Checked the texture of the soil. Estimated the need for water. Planted seeds. And when the weather seemed right, I began to sow. Whatever followed has been due to the farmer's sweat and luck and providential benediction. The crop is yours to see. Whatever seems good comes from the earth and the seed – the blemishes are mine ...

❦

To capture the expanse of *Zindaginama*, it was important to get close to the dialects. Folk languages and dialects draw their strength from the soil, they face life with a rustic belligerence. Nurturing the collective psyche with their dusky earthiness, they remain a part of literature.

The truth is that regional languages and dialects are quite capable of defending their rights. They can easily handle the allegations of encroachment made against them by Hindi from its lofty perch. We should not forget that the Hindi reader speaks not just in Hindi, nor will she be trapped for long within the walls of regionalism.

A complete Indian has now been born. She will surely vault over petty parochialism. This is the reader who will hope for and expect a lot more from Hindi than its translated façade of linguistic purity or the majestic grace of a language assaulted by Sanskrit.

❦

The *Zindaginama* season was long. The earthy fragrance of the village wafted through many winters and summers.

This piece was first published in Hindi as "Chand Notes Zindaginama Par" in *Sobti Ek Sohbat*, an anthology of selections from her work, Rajkamal Prakashan, 1989.

And get-togethers kept my house bustling.

Chacha Fateh Ali, Kamailaahi, Ganda Singh, Mauladaad, Jahadaad Khan, Gurditt Singh, Taaya, Maiya Singh, Munshi Ilmuddin, Tufail Singh, Maul Mirasi, Kokala Doda, Hira Sansi, Chachi, Mahri Maa, Bibi, Bebe Karbhari, Shahji, Shahni, and Rabayaan who loves to rhyme. This crowd, full of easy simplicity and human warmth, took a shape of its own, like a giant, deep-rooted tree growing out of the earth.

I carried a hope in my heart that the people who disappeared in the ruins of history of a divided country could be brought to life, in flesh and blood. That they would seem living – not lifeless like portraits but complete with thick, dark coloured clothes and personalities with grainy textures.

I am a part of that crowd. I am one of them. Or else, putting on urban airs, I would have transplanted their coarse ways and rough speech into contemporary, cultured idioms to create a more readable interpretation of their lifestyle ...

❦

A few ordinary questions

Can a novel be written without dialogue?

Should a novel be written without dialogue?

Should not words borrowed from dialects be used in dialogue to establish the authenticity of the characters and their environment?

Should dialogues, in the tradition of middle-class civility, be set only in semi-literary language?

Should the diction of dialogues be close to cultured declamation?

When translated from English, should dialogues be presented only in "intellectual-sounding" Hindi?

Is there a standard language for dialogue in Hindi?

Even if there is, should not the glory of the dialogue be preserved by using the open, unadorned language of the common person?

A large part of the world's population, being illiterate, has long expressed itself only through the spoken word. Assuming that there is a realm of the literary language separate from that of the spoken language, is there a need for checks on writers who use the spoken word to present characters?

Would we like to remember that the folk literature and poetry of any country in the world has its origin in the oral tradition – with no help of a written language?

We also know, that in our extensive human heritages folk literature and poetry are capable of matching any timeless literary creations.

Then, is there any need to defend the "literary" culture of literature?

❦

A poem instead of a preface

One night, I sat and with surprising simplicity, in a chain of words, wrote a long piece.

I knew it was not poetry, but whenever I read the piece it would clarify my relationship with the novel.

It assured me about my surroundings and made me indifferent to certain all-consuming attachments. Reading it, my emotional perspective shifted from nostalgia (it was centered on this piece) and I grew alert to the sound of big collisions.

This piece was particularly significant because through it I was able to "delink" myself from the present. This was a difficult process. I would like to believe that the association between me and the piece was intense but formal.

The piece would act difficult, and I would often plan to keep it away.

Then it was time for *Zindaginama* to go to press. The moment of decision approached – the decision to send or not to send it with the novel. I read it again, gave it a fresh look. This first piece was about getting away from it. That seemed to decide its destiny. According to me, it was impossible to keep it in.

I left the final decision to Sheela Sandhu.

I am sending you a long piece. It was the primary reason for my writing this book. It may not be appropriate for others to read. I am neutral to its addition to the novel. I will agree with your decision on this, whatever it be.

I was happy to see it in *Zindaginama*. The publisher had managed to preserve a fragile bond.

An evening : 28 August, 1974

Nainital during monsoons. Offseason. Far from the bustle. Damp solitude. Lights shimmering in a few rooms. The lake, outside, shrouded in a rainy darkness.

I sit in the verandah as the August evening sets.
Rain dripping on the tin roof,
Rain drops on the green waves in the lake.
Gusts of wind. A cloudburst.
The mountains ahead turn dark.

Cumulus showers, playful, naughty.
Clouds of mist float as mirrors across the lake.
The wind, the rain, the rumbling of clouds.
I descend with my raincoat. Shocks of waves on the lake.
I waft in the air, plunge and emerge from the tarn of Time.
I have become new. Twenty years younger.
No breaks in my past
The moment and I, we are one.
I run along the edge of the path.
It rains harder. And harder.
Roaring thunder.
Floods of lightning.
Silent mountains tremble, they quake.
Without pause, I dash.

My red umbrella flips in the wind.
I want to soak and soak in the rain,
to water the wastelands of my soul.
I am a desert, not a garden.
A sailboat in the middle of the lake staggers to the shore,
bobbing, inching.
I avoid a glance, embracing my heart,
the path beyond the lake.
Unknowingly, I bet with myself – a run around the lake.
A gale, a storm, whatever it be.
Even death, to capture this stormy evening in my soul.
My body is the earth, my heart the sky, and tangled into my feet,
this evening is my destiny.
A gentle rhythmic run, unhurried.
Why should I rush
now that I have decided that I must get there?
I shrink with my strides.
And grow.
I appear for a moment, then disappear. Lost.
You are no more –
No! I am.
I buy new shoes before returning to my room.
The fireplace has been lit, for my wet clothes and me.
A change of clothes. I sit on the floor,
order for food, and await the reward for getting soaked.
A tune plays in my heart.
This evening, this moment, I share an intimacy
with me, my body and soul. I am with myself.
A sound –
old or new?
None.
A pain –
seen or unseen?
No.

An affection –
blossoming, shattering?
No.
Nothing at all.
I sit in the room. Time sits with me.
A Time all my own.
A glance flies across to the table.
A heap of papers, next to them a rose?
A gift from the gardener. perhaps ...
Flowerbeds made of paper, paperbeds.
I take another flower from the vase,
wipe the stem and place it next to the rose.
A blossom gifted from me to Time.
The rains pause.
A handful of crimson from the setting sun
smeared across the window pane.
I stand still, next to the table. Still, for a long while.
Not a scratch in my heart. No joy, no sorrow.
No anguish, no ecstasy. Just a quiet waiting ...

I open and wipe my pen. Fill it with ink.
Bend over the blank sheets. A flash of childhood memories!
I see my village, and in my ears rise the echoes
Allah-o-Akbar
Allah-o-Akbar
Allah-o-Akbar
Allah-o-Akbar
Ashadullah Ilaah Ilalallah
Ashadullah Ilaah Ilalallah
Ashaduann Muhammadarrasulalallah
Ashaduann Muhammadarrasulalallah

With this echo began *Zindaginama*.

A morning : 28 January, 1979

Three-thirty at night.
It is almost dawn.
A sense of being parted from a long season.
My room was bustling through the night
Munching raisins, I reach the edge of the sea in my thoughts .
I stand on the sand. Water all around.
Sand here, water there.
I nervously bite into an apple.
Mummy reads me, as only she can ...
Tea?
Ji.
She walks towards the kitchen, but her attention
hovers about me.
Every writer needs a perennial brook
that never dries up.
After tea, I am on the last lines of *Zindaginama* :
chun kaar aj hamaa halite darguzasht
halaalast budarn ba shamshir dast
When all else fails, lifting the sword against oppression is justified.

I speak it aloud. Repeat it.
Sensations overwhelm my being –
to fight injustice,
to struggle valiantly.

The Crafting Years

1925 Born on February 18, in Gujarat, a village in West Punjab (now in Pakistan).

1944 Her first story, "Lama," is published in *Vichar.*

1948 She serves as a governess to the family of Tej Singh, the then Maharaja of Sirohi, Mount Abu.

1950 She is appointed Principal of the Army Officers' Children's School in Delhi.

1952 She joins the Delhi Administration as an editor in the Department of Adult Literacy.

1954 She receives a prize for "Dadi Amma" in *The Hindustan Times* International Short Story Competition.

1957 She attends the Regional UNESCO workshop in Burma and produces *The Prince of Peace* (on the Buddha).

1968 *Mitro Marjani* is published – and causes an instant stir.

1979 "Badalon ke Ghere" is dramatized. *Mitro Marjani* is adapted for the stage.

1980 The Sahitya Akademi Award is conferred on her for *Zindaginama.* The first woman to be awarded for Hindi. She resigns her job to devote herself more fully to writing. Punjabi University honours her with a Fellowship.

1981 She receives the Shiromani Award.

1982 She is invited to be the Writer-in-Residence at the Nirala Srijan Peeth in Bhopal. She receives the Hindi Academy Award. *Daar se Bichhudi* is dramatized.

1986 She becomes a consultant to the TV serial, *Buniyaad.*

1988 The National School of Drama produces *Mitro Marjani* It runs a record 67 shows.

1991 *Ai Ladki,* a novella based on her mother's life, is published.

1993 *Dil-o-Danish* published, once again by Rajkamal Prakashan, her publishers since 1958.

1996 Awarded the prestigious Sahitya Akademi Fellowship.

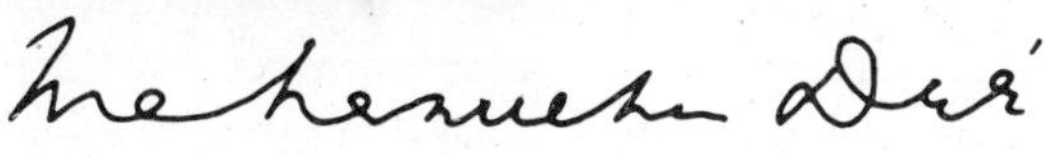

MAHASVETA DEVI

"I am a woman,
and I am writing.
but I am not
writing of women
alone. What I am
writing ... is about
class exploitation."
– Mahasveta Devi

Here is a person who firmly believes that every writer should have a social conscience, and that writers are answerable to people. So, even at seventy, she insists, "I'm connected to work, to activity. So much mechanical work is done by hands ... I believe in hands."

Mahasveta Devi's creed clearly is a single-word one – action! Social activism and a committed political agenda, it is often said, do not make for good creative writing. For, where does ideology leave off and "literature" begin? But for Mahasveta Devi, there has never been a conflict of interest as far as the two are concerned. "All work – my active work, my creative writing, any journal editing, or journalistic writing – all these are inter-supplementary."

As she says in an interview with Sue Dickman, "Throughout my books, I see history ... People's history ... Being close to indigenous people does not mean that I cannot write about them." A firm believer in documentation, much of her fiction is based on an extensive reading of the history of Bengal and on her work in rural Bengal, Bihar and Orissa. Her first book to be published, *Jhansir Rani*, was a meticulously-researched, carefully-reconstructed biography of Laxmibai, the queen of Jhansi and one of the leaders of the Revolt of 1857. "Facts, statistics, and data talk much more in my opinion than what you *think* about events," says Mahasveta Devi. Other sources for her writing are oral folklore, Vividh Bharati radio and Shahrukh Khan films!

Mahasveta Devi was born in Dhaka on January 14, 1926, to Manish Ghatak, a poet and novelist, and Dharitri Devi, a writer and social worker. About her family she says, "I was fortunate to be born in a family where both sides were very liberal and women were held in great respect. The women were terrors, indomitable, fearless ... And all received education. At home we were nine brothers and sisters ... every day was a festival, so much sharing, I don't see that now. This had a great influence on my work, on my life. I love people."

She went to schools in Midnapore and Calcutta and graduated in English from Shantiniketan in 1946. Her master's in English was completed seventeen years later. She grew up in a time of great upheaval. The Quit India Movement of 1942 was followed in Bengal by the horrible famine of 1943. Then came the horrors of the Partition and the unrest caused by the Tebhaga peasant movement led by the Communist Party – Mahasveta Devi's involvement with social and political happenings started early.

After her marriage to Bijon Bhattacharya, the noted playwright, she worked for a while as a clerk in the Post and Telegraph Department,

---

"I am a ..." is from a conversation with Sue Dickman, *The Book Review*, April 1995.

but lost her job as she was suspected of being a Communist. In a long and chequered career, she has been a schoolteacher, a dealer in soap dyes, a failed exporter of monkeys and a roving reporter for rural Bengal for the daily *Jugantar.*

Her writing career began with the occasional piece in the weekly *Sachitra Bharat,* for which she used the pseudonym, "Sumitra Devi." In 1956, she became a professional writer – "I wrote a lot, even potboilers, trash, but I'm not ashamed because they brought in money," she recalls now. In 1970, *Aranyer Adhikar* brought her to the fore as a writer to be reckoned with. A Sahitya Akademi Award winning work, this novel has been described by Manabendra Bandhopadhyay, the critic, as "savage, fecund, irresistible." It has been translated into almost all major Indian languages. What she is really happy about is that it was translated into Ho and other tribal languages of Eastern India and she is proud that it led to a "tremendous upsurge among the tribals."

While talking of the savage humour that often characterizes her work, Mahasveta Devi feels that the tragedy of Indian writing is that it is too full of profundity. Like Bhupen Khakhar she believes that Indians do not know how to laugh at themselves. All questions about the craft of writing are consistently dismissed by Mahasveta Devi as "faltu things." Her standard answer is "I do not have any brain, I have only brawn."

Not too concerned with the technical aspects of writing, Mahasveta Devi is on the look out for her ideal "reader" – "If the writer works so hard, then the reader must also work hard to understand the writer." It is hardly surprising then that she is disappointed with the lack of perceptive readers and critics!

"I consider myself an Indian writer because what I am writing could be true of any part of India," she further asserts. This writer who refuses to be classified as only a Bangla writer, characteristically regards her works as being true to the lives of indigenous people all over the world, which is why she encourages translations of her writing.

It would be difficult to encapsulate in a few lines her thirty years of social activism. She has worked extensively for the liberation of bonded labourers by writing journalistic pieces in journals ranging from the *Economic and Political Weekly* and *Business Standard* to *Bartaman* and *Jugantar*. She has founded and is associated with innumerable welfare organizations in Bihar and Bengal.

For Mahasveta Devi, not being a man has never been an issue. She acknowledges the validity of the women's position, women's thought, but maintains that her work focuses on "class exploitation" in which "the underclass is exploited – both men and women." Her fiction too chronicles the "silent revolution" she has been a witness to, and indeed been instrumental in bringing about, in the fifteen-thousand strong tribal community of Purulia, a district in West Bengal.

"I am the product of my times, my historical background, my family, my education," she says. The present day, Mahasveta Devi continues to be surrounded by her times and society, she has not taken refuge in the proverbial ivory tower. Even at 70, each and every minute of her time is taken up in meeting people, answering correspondence, travelling to interior West Bengal. At the time of this volume's going to press, Mahasveta Devi was in New Delhi for a meet of five hundred NGOs to look at the voluntary sector, its role and impact. There she reiterated her stand of half a century. "Go to the people, to learn from them, not only teach. In the forties, as Communists we believed that Revolution was lurking behind the lamp post, and we only had to usher it in. But now I know that we have to work for transformation to occur – and work within the system."

Has a life spent in social work resulted in a neglect of Mahasveta the writer? She confesses, "Even now, sixteen hours of my day are devoted to penning things other than literature. I have harmed Mahasveta the writer the most." This, after 41 novels, 15 short story collections, one play, five children's stories, two historical biographies, and innumerable newspaper articles – a body of work that neither Time nor readers can ignore. Nor can we ignore what the noted writer Kamala Das once said about her: "Mahasveta Devi ... is a wonderful, fearless woman. She has learned of the tribals, she has lived with them, and she's dealing with material she's acquainted with. Write about her. Make a cult out of her."

MAHASVETA DEVI

in conversation with
Enakshi Chatterjee

I knew that Mahasveta Devi lives in a boarding house near Ballygunj Station. A new overbridge now connects the busy Rashbehari Avenue with a developing stretch of land, finally leading to the Eastern Metropolitan Bypass. The overbridge is called Bijon Setu, in memory of a brave young man, Bijon, who gave his life trying to save his fellow passengers in a train compartment from armed dacoits. But, for someone living in Ballygunj Station Road, this bridge is not much of a boon. I realized this as the taxi was obliged to take a winding route below the bridge, inching its way through a confusion of pedestrians, cyclists, autorickshaws, vegetable and fruit vendors and people loitering about. The place was teeming with activities. Just the place for a writer like Mahasveta Devi .

Finding the house was no problem. As I passed Ballygunj Station, all the hustle and bustle came to a stop in front of a sprawling house in which Mahasveta Devi occupies a set of rooms. I had forgotten to ask her which floor she was on, and was debating whether to go and look at the letter boxes, when I heard her calling me from upstairs. "This way," she said, pointing to a spiral staircase. It wasn't an easy climb, balancing my umbrella, my shoulder bag and the saree. "Is that the way you negotiate it?" I asked her.

"Of course," she said. "I climb much faster than you do. Do you see that room?" She showed me a locked door a few steps below.

"How do you get into that room?"

"You have to climb over the railings, of course."

"I don't think I would like to do that," I said.

"Too bad," said Mahasveta, "but just in case you wish to buy some tribal artefacts, I can get you something for less than a hundred rupees."

"How about that interview, Mahasveta?" I came to the point, and she said "Come right in."

I went through a passage to a room which seemed to be her bedroom-cum-workplace. Piles of papers, books, files lay scattered everywhere. "Sit on the bed, if you don't mind." I didn't have much choice. Besides, this seemed more informal. She offered me tea. "But you will have to take it black. I don't take milk or sugar."

Midway through the interview, I asked her if I should leave now and come back some other time. "I have taken up a lot of your time already. I don't want to keep you from your work." To which she protested, "But this is also work. Let us get on with it."

She seemed quite happy to talk about her writing, but I could see that she was keen to enquire about my family, our common friends, particularly my children who, at one time used to be very fond of Mahamashi. Yet she could also be very business-like. "Let us stick to your questions. We can get together again for a friendly chat."

The interview went on. I was dying for another cup of tea or a cold drink but did not want to bother her. Evidently she lived in spartan austerity, working, as she has confessed in the interview, ten to twelve hours a day. Perhaps she is never hungry or thirsty. I looked around to see what she did to relax. Files stacked on files greeted my eyes. It was a very severe-looking room.

At one time she looked up and smiled. "You know I feel quite amused. ..."

"What on earth for?" I asked.

"It is just that I am not used to receiving visitors like you – a well-dressed person with a gold chain, eartops, bangles – ha, ha."

I was offended now. "You know very well that this is what I usually wear. I can't help being what I am."

We parted the best of friends. I was reminded of the Mahasveta I used to know, who was not yet so taken up with the cause of the tribals, and of the wonderful times we used to have, of the tremendous success of a programme we had initiated once, to felicitate six old time stalwarts – Santa Devi, Sita Devi, Punyalata Chakravarty, Giribala Devi and Shailabala Ghoshjaya – and of the overwhelming public response! I was also reminded of the many lunches we used to have together with Chitra Ghosh, Gouri Ayub and Shyamashree Lal.

Those were the days!

EC: *When did you start writing, Mahasveta ?*

MD: I am not counting what I wrote for school magazines. My first book was published in 1956 – *Jhansir Rani*. The motivation for writing this historical biography came from within. I visited all the places the Rani had been to and collected plenty of oral material. I discovered that the oral tradition is a very valuable source of history. What struck me about my subject was her youth. She had led an uprising in Central India – it was really a peoples' uprising. She was non-communal. Her closest soldiers were Pathans and Afghans. I thought that was a very striking fact.

The book sold well. It helped me considerably. After that I became a professional writer – I had to write to make a living.

***EC:** What do you think you would have been if you had decided not to be a writer?*

MD: You see, I have tried my hand at various jobs. I worked hard to be a schoolteacher. For a year I was at the Ramesh Mitra Institution on a leave vacancy. If they had kept me on, I would have stayed a teacher and retired as one. Then I also worked as a clerk in a Central Government office from 1949 to 1950. I was sacked for being a Communist.

***EC:** Were you?*

MD: I have never been a party member. My husband Bijon was, for a while. He was one of the founder members of the IPTA. His famous play, *Nabanna,* was set in the background of the Famine. K A Abbas based his *Dharti ke Lal* on this play. In the fifties, we went to Bombay. We stayed in Andheri with Santi Bardhan of Little Ballet Troupe.

I CAME FROM A FAIRLY AFFLUENT BACKGROUND. MY FIRST EXPOSURE TO POVERTY AND MISERY CAME AFTER MY MARRIAGE.

I came from a fairly affluent background. My first exposure to poverty and misery came after my marriage and it changed the direction of my life. That was my first brush with Communism too. I had great respect for the parent CPI organization (not the present CPI) and their movements. I still go to visit Kansari Haldar, one of the legendary leaders of the Tebhaga peasant movement.

***EC:** Do you have to juggle writing with other commitments?*

MD: Oh yes! I have always been doing many other kinds of work. For instance, I was one of the founders of the Palamau District Bonded Labour Organisation which was set up in 1980. Then there were the domestic chores to finish. We were very poor so there was no getting away from housework, though I don't think that kept me from writing.

***EC:** You don't think being a woman makes it more difficult ...*

MD: That's nonsense!

***EC:** How did you feel when your first book was published?*

MD: Happy, naturally. You see, I never take anything for granted. There is a part of me which always remains detached and objective. For instance, I was sent to Geneva to represent India at the summit on the Economic Advancement of Rural Women in the Third World. It was a great honour. Yet I knew I'd have to come back to work.

***EC:** What are your feelings about trying to get a work published? Do rejection slips put you off?*

MD: I wouldn't know about that because all my work is commissioned. There were only three exceptions – *Jhansir Rani*, *Boshai Tudu* and *Chotti Munda* – I *had* to write them. They came spontaneously. As for rejection slips, I think the literary market in Bengal at least does not operate that way. There isn't that much of a gap between writing and publishing. Editors, rejection slips – these are Western concepts. They don't apply here.

***EC:** What about the response to your work? Has it ever come as a surprise? Do you pay much attention to reviews? Who is your best critic?*

MD: As far as my writing goes, you rarely find a serious review in Bangla as you do in Hindi and the other languages. Objective criticism vanished from the Bangla literary scene after Sudhin Dutt's

Parichay. I do regard myself as my best critic. I instinctively know which of my writings will pass the test and which won't. And I have written a lot of no-goods. That too, I know.

***EC:** Many writers feel the need to withdraw from their surroundings? Is that true of you too?*

MD: No. On the contrary, I get involved completely. My work is not isolated from my environment.

***EC:** Do you like meeting other writers, critics, readers at seminars? Do you ever feel the need to discuss your work at a public forum, or would you rather let it do all the talking?*

MD: I try my best to avoid seminars etc. Still, at times, I have to attend them. I can only respond to someone who understands me totally and has been reading my work for many years. Usually, people judge me on the merit of one book or a particular type of book. For example, those who know me only as the writer of *Hajar Churasir Ma* call me "a revolutionary."

***EC:** That's unfair!*

MD: I think so too. It pains me. Since I seldom come across serious readers, I feel quite cut-off. Now I refuse to give autographs to people who have not read me seriously. Yes, ultimately I think my books speak for themselves.

***EC:** What are your political leanings?*

MD: Though I am a Left-winger, I am not affiliated to any party. I think my political agenda is more than evident in my writing.

> OBJECTIVE CRITICISM VANISHED FROM THE BANGLA LITERARY SCENE AFTER SUDHIN DUTT'S *PARICHAY*.

***EC:** What do you feel about "protest" literature?*

MD: I don't believe in labelling writing. Writers of an earlier generation – people like Jyotirmoyee Devi, Ashapurna Devi, Shailabala Ghoshjaya – all of them have explored the position of women in society and have documented the need for protest. Ashapurna, in particular. She too was an activist in her own way. But that Ashapurna is yet to be given a proper evaluation, yet to be discovered. Just because her novels sold well, were adapted for films, plays, TV serials, she was labelled "a popular writer." As though popular literature can't be good literature. As for myself, I believe in presenting facts, not in airing my views. Documentation is very important. I've been doing that in *Bartika*, the journal I edit.

EC: *Documentation on tribals?*

MD: More than that. I am trying hard, through writing, to document as much of the past as I can. The year before last I wrote a novel set in eleventh-century Bengal for the Puja issue of a magazine. I have also written about Bengal of the sixteenth and eighteenth centuries. These are not just tribal histories.

EC: *I am reminded of some of your stories for children, stories like* Nei Nagarer Sei Raja *which is set in the time of Warren Hastings. And that extremely powerful novel* Kabi Bandyaghati Gyanir Jiban O Mrityu *which is set some time in the past.*

MD: There you are! I try hard to remain faithful to history.

EC: *The result is a very fine blend of history and fiction.*

MD: *Andhar Manik* seems to be your favourite. I could not have written that novel if I did not know the period details, rituals, folklore, customs.

EC: *Most of your novels are meticulously researched. Do you get somebody else to do your research?*

MD: No. I do it myself. In fact now I can feel the pulse of the people. This has come from experience. It works both ways. Direct experience leads to an instinctive understanding.

EC: *Do you write in any other language?*

MD: Yes, I write in English when necessary or when I am asked to. But all my creative work is in Bangla.

***EC:** What do you like to read? Any favourites? Influences?*

MD: History fascinates me. Whenever possible, I study data, statistics, government gazetteers, human rights laws, laws regarding tribals. In the last twenty years I haven't had the time to read much fiction and I have never been a reader of poetry. My life has changed course, so have my priorities. There are few books I would like to reread.

I have always been a voracious reader. My mother made me read old Bangla classics when I was young. They were not easy to read. But she would insist, "Read them now, you won't have time for them later." She was absolutely right.

All that disciplined reading during my adolescent years laid the groundwork for the writer in me. That was when I was introduced to the sixteenth-century poet Mukundaram and his *Kabikankan Chandi*. I liked his use of language, his description of common people, tribals, the contemporary social scene, everything. I owe much to him. Only him, no one else.

ASHAPURNA WAS LABELLED "A POPULAR WRITER." AS THOUGH POPULAR LITERATURE CAN'T BE GOOD LITERATURE.

***EC:** In the delightful novel,* Bioscoper Baksha (The Bioscope Box), *which is quite a departure from your other work, one finds a slight touch of the Lila Majumdar style – fantasy, nostalgia, part autobiography. Would you agree?*

MD: Could be, I wasn't aware of it. I have read and enjoyed Lila Majumdar greatly. Do you know something? Nobody took notice of *Bioscoper Baksha*. But Samaresh Basu said that it was the best novel of that Puja season. I was glad to hear that.

***EC:** Do you read other writers when you are working on a particular book?*

MD: No, never. I don't read fiction then. All my work, in varying degrees, is based on research.

***EC:** About your writing habits – do you have some kind of a routine?*

MD: Twenty years ago I could have sorted out one. Now I am so hard pressed for time that I write whenever I can. I try to maintain a 10-12 hours a day work schedule. "Stanadayini" was written in one day. "Draupadi" too.

***EC:** So Mahasveta the activist is eating into the time of Mahasveta the writer?*

MD: You are trying to label me again. I have always been involved in various things – right from the days of famine relief work in 1944. People come to me with their grievances, seeking help. My creative work, journalism, activism and magazine editing – they sustain one another.

***EC:** About writing, where does a story begin – with a line, an idea, an image?*

MD: I really don't know. A lot of thought and planning goes into my major writing. I have a habit of jotting down words, phrases, anything which strikes me. Sometimes I write down the points of a story without knowing what will come out of it. Often that story does not get written at all. Anyway, after I begin writing, the story often takes a course I had not intended.

***EC:** How many drafts do you require?*

MD: The first is the final draft.

***EC:** Have you ever revised stories after they have been published?*

MD: The stories for the Puja numbers are always written in a hurry. So revision is necessary. I normally don't make major changes. But, in *Hajar Churasir Ma,* I rewrote an entire chapter.

EC: *Do you ever find yourself repeating names, situations? Do you have certain preferences when it comes to creating characters?*

MD: Yes, in the context of Palamau . Otherwise, No. I treat Palamau as a mirror for India. I have lived among the tribals, loved them, worked with them. I have been saying to the Government, to people all over India that you must give the tribals the respect they deserve. Just allotting some funds is not enough – the money does not reach them. To cut a long story short it is because of my involvement with the tribals that they also appear as characters in my stories. And I keep going back to them just to see what they are doing.

EC: *So you are obsessed with your tribal characters?*

MD: Obsessed? Yes, you could call it that. But you know me so well Enakshi, need I tell you that the sense of duty is an obsession with me. I think I have a duty towards society – every creative writer should have a social conscience.

> I AM SO HARD PRESSED FOR TIME. "STANADAYINI" WAS WRITTEN IN ONE DAY. "DRAUPADI" TOO.

EC: *Yes, I have noticed that when we were doing* Ananda Path *– a series of graded Bangla primers for Anglo-Indian schools. Total dedication was needed to do a thorough job and you did give it more than your best. I'm sorry if I have offended you. To go back to the original question – Involvement with characters: is it painful when the time comes to part company?*

MD: I was very involved with *Nati* which incidentally is my first published novel – *Jhansir Rani* was not a novel. Yes, parting company was painful. I would say the same thing about *Andhar Manik*. Generally speaking, after writing a story, I need some time to get it out of my system.

***EC:** What type of narrative voice do you prefer?*

MD: The third person.

***EC:** Have you ever experimented with forms like the epic?*

MD: Not really. I have used a vast canvas and epic material in *Amrita Sanchay*, and in *Andhar Manik*.

***EC:** Is there any particular symbol or myth that you often use?*

MD: Elephants. They appear again and again, and not just in the tribal context. You see elephants stand for things ancient – valued, but moving towards extinction. Water is another symbol I use frequently.

***EC:** What do you feel about forms like the fable and the allegory?*

MD: Fables, folklore, riddles, rituals, death-rites – all are very important. Let me tell you of an interesting incident. It was during one hot summer in Bihar, in the Singhbhum district. After walking what seemed like miles and miles, I told the tribals that another twenty-mile trek in the heat would kill me. They reassured me, "If you die we will get big boulders from far to put on your grave." For them that was the highest honour – to bring boulders from a distance, not use the locally available stones. It was the greatest respect they could have accorded me.

***EC:** Haven't you used myth in* Pterodactyl, Puran Sahay O Pritha?

MD: *Pterodactyl,* now that is a myth – my entire tribal experience has gone into it. My effort has been to use the symbol to focus on the situation of the entire tribal community in India.

***EC:** What else do you write beside stories?*

MD: Novels, plays adapted from stories, children's fiction, text books, journalistic pieces, newspaper columns ...

***EC:** Anything else that you would like to write some day?*

MD: My autobiography.

***EC:** Do you encourage translations? Have you ever translated any of your work?*

MD: Yes, I think they are important. My books have been translated into many Indian languages. Except for those in Hindi, I have no means of checking their authenticity and faithfulness. But Vikraman Nair told me the Malayalam translations are excellent. I have translated some of my own work, but not much.

***EC:** Have any of your stories been filmed?*

MD: Yes. *Sangharsh* (with Dilip Kumar) and *Rudali* in Hindi, *Behula* and *Janani* in Bangla. They have won awards.

***EC:** So how do you feel about them?*

MD: I don't know, I have mixed feelings. *Rudali,* the film, has almost no connection with my story. The stage version, performed by the Rangakarmee group in Hindi, was totally faithful.

***EC:** Have you considered adapting some of your work for screen? Would you, if you were asked to?*

MD: No, I wouldn't. That's for professionals.

***EC:** One last question, Mahasveta. What do you consider the "dharma" of a writer?*

MD: I can speak only for myself: To do my best, no compromises in the process. In whatever I undertake to do, I ask myself, Am I doing my best?

***EC:** So the writer's "dharma" is to write, as Sri Krishna said to Arjuna.*

MD: Oh, come on!

IN WHATEVER I UNDERTAKE TO DO, I ASK MYSELF, AM I DOING MY BEST?

This is an extract from another conversation with Mahasveta Devi. On July 13, 1995, Babli Moitra Saraf and Frederica Oddera met her in the same set of three minuscule rooms in Calcutta. The morning papers had reported the demise of Ashapurna Devi, the grande dame of Bangla literature. "She taught us to wield the pen unto the last breath," recalled Mahasveta Devi. Yet in her own life Mahasveta has gone beyond the world of the pen. Action is her byword. Enveloped in the warmth of her personality and mugs of hot tea, Babli and Frederica talked to her about her life and beliefs.

B&F: *Your childhood and youth, your family ...?*

MD: I was fortunate to be born in a family where both sides were very liberal and women were held in great respect. The women were terrors, indomitable, fearless ... I attended school in Shantiniketan when Tagore was still alive. It was a great place where girls and boys from all over the country came. We could do everything together – jump into the river, climb trees, play hockey and football.

B&F: *And after Shantiniketan?*

MD: Bengal at that time was very different. So much was happening then ... the Bengal Famine, when I saw hunger from very close quarters, people dying on Calcutta streets, bodies piled up. I was a member of the Communist Student Organization. Then the struggle for Independence. On my mother's side there were so many "terrorists." In 1942, there were the cyclone and Quit India. In 1946, the riots of Calcutta, in 1947 – the Partition. After the Partition, the Communist Party led peasant movements – the Tebhaga. All these were part of my life ...

B&F: *What would you count as literary influences on your work?*

MD: I don't think any writer has directly influenced me. But I grew up amidst writers. My father, Manish Ghatak, was a pathbreaker. He wrote about the Calcutta slums and used a certain "cockney" language. In the 60s, I discovered Kabi Mukundaram Chakroborty, who borrows language from anywhere, any walk of life. I too borrow from everywhere – from oral traditions, proverbs, folk customs, rituals, whatever.

I watch Shahrukh Khan films whenever I can. And all my major books have been written with a transistor playing Vividh Bharati. A tree you put in good soil will thrive, but you'll also find some which feed on absolute rubbish and survive somehow. I'm like that.

B&F: *Where would you place yourself in the Bangla literary tradition?*

MD: I am off the mainstream, also off the sidestream. ... I'm considered a menace. I think of myself in Jim Corbett's words, "not a menace ... just an outsized man leopard." In my writing, you'll find a lot of savage, black humour. The tragedy of Indian writing is that it is full of profundity and Indians do not know how to laugh at themselves.

B&F: *Do you think about the craft of writing?*

MD: I don't think about it at all, you know. Where is time for faltu things. I do not have any brain, I have only brawn. When do I think about my craft? This woman (*a destitute lady who had come to her for refuge)* has to be sent home. The boys working there have to be given lunch. *(Shabar boys running an outlet for tribal handicrafts.)*

B&F: *Gayatri Chakravarty Spivak defines your language as "an extraordinary mélange of street slang, the dialect of East Bengal, the everyday household language of family and servant, and the occasional gravity of elegant Bengali." Why do you choose such a stratified language?*

MD: It has to be that way. If the writer works so hard then the reader must also work hard to understand the writer. Ofcourse, I also write a lot of easy reading but not all the time. You see, whatever happens, I want to remain answerable to myself at the end of the day.

ARJUN

translated by
Mridula Nath Chakraborty

Aghrayan was almost over and the month of Poush was just round the corner. It was not cold enough yet for the sun's warmth to be welcome.

The ripe paddy crop in Bishal Mahato's farm had been harvested the previous day. All day, along with the harvesters and casual grain pickers, Ketu Shabar too had been collecting the leftover grains of paddy in the fields. Now, in the foggy twilight, he needed a little liquor to warm him and to relax his aching body. The desire was sure to remain ungratified, but, he told himself, there was no harm in fantasizing.

His wife, Mohoni, was not with him. She came to the fields only when he was not around – Ketu was frequently in and out of jails. His offence – clearing the jungles for the paddy crop.

It was no use trying to reason with Ketu Shabar about this. Ram Haldar gave him the job and Ketu did it. Haldar collected the profits from the felled trees, and Ketu and others like him went to jail. But what could he do? All that mattered was the four pice at the end of the day – be it for chopping down a tree or chopping up a man. In fact, it might be easier to chop up a man! Why hadn't anyone asked him to do that? wondered Ketu. He might even earn four whole rupees that way! But he quickly corrected himself – I didn't mean it seriously, of course.

❦

Ketu does not ever question his predicament. If you were born in the Shabar tribe of Purulia, you *had* to cut down the trees. And you *had* to go to jail. It could be no other way. If one Ketu was in jail, and something needed to be done, Haldar could always find another Ketu. Nothing lost – except that, the woman in the house had to go looking for work.

The last time Ketu had been jailed for cutting down the trees of the Forest Department, Mohoni had gone out looking for work. And who knows what happened ... In spite of the inevitability of the situation, Ketu couldn't face the prospect of returning to an empty hut. No wonder the mind and the body demanded liquor. A little intoxication, a little oblivion ...

Lost in reverie, Ketu was suddenly confronted by Bishal Mahato. "I have some work for you," he said.

"Is it about the votes, babu?"

"No, no! I'm not worried about that. The people will have to elect whoever I nominate, won't they?"

"Hanh, babu."

"Arjun" was first published in Bangla in the *Dainik Bartaman*, 1984. This story has been translated exclusively for Katha.

"Well? What did Ram Haldar tell you?"

"The same thing that you said."

"And what was your reply?"

"Just what I told you."

"What kind of an answer is that?"

"I am just a fool, babu," said Ketu.

"Never mind. There is something I want you to do. Are you interested?"

❦

Ram Haldar and Bishal Mahato belonged to different parties. But for Ketu and his companions, they were two of a kind. One had to appear dumb whenever they were around. Both these deities had to be pleased, if one were to make a living in this area. But who among them would dare to say "No" to these party members? Haldar and Mahato too knew that the Shabars were indispensable – they held the world record for jail terms, after all.

Now, Bishal Mahato had indeed managed to arouse Ketu's curiosity. Elections were round the corner. Bishal babu had been busy – attending meetings, giving speeches. So if the matter didn't concern votes, what could it possibly be? Whatever it was, it must be something shady.

"You have to cut down the arjun tree," Bishal said.

"Why, babu?" Ketu was startled.

"Just do what I say."

"Please babu, I've just come out of jail, babu."

"If I wanted to send you back, would you be able to prevent it?" asked Bishal Mahato.

"No, babu."

"This is not like one of Ram Haldar's contracts. Only through his illegal operations do you land in jail. Who'd dare to arrest you if I ordered the removal of the tree from the main intersection at the government road?"

Ketu's mind went blank. He had never thought about it, but it was true. You worked for Ram Haldar and you promptly got caught. That meant another trip to the jail. But Bishal babu's word was law. He actually ran the country, you know! So, who would send you to jail if, under his instructions, the shady tree no longer stood at the government road?

An idea flashed through Ketu's mind. "Babu, are you making a pucca road this time, to ensure the votes?"

"Pucca road? Here? Ketu, you must be mad! It has not happened in thirty years. And it won't happen now. No, I need the tree."

"A full grown tree?"

"Yes, the whole arjun tree."

"And how would you transport it?"

"Ram babu's truck, what else."

It was as if the clear sky, the pure, cold, air and the Santoshi Ma bhajans blaring out on the cassette player were prompting Bishal Mahato to speak the truth.

❦

It was that magical hour when earth bids farewell to the day and twilight disappears into the arms of night. The wind carried the smell of ripe paddy from the fields of Bandihi. But Ketu was oblivious to all that. Mahato's request had stunned him. It was as if a huge stone had been placed on his chest. This is what Chandra Santhal must have felt when, during the harvest revolution, they had pinned him down with a half-maund measure. That weight ... Frightening.

Bishal Mahato and Ram Haldar belonged to two different parties. But only in word did they represent opposite camps. One conducted the Panchayat, the other ran the sawmill just outside the borders of the district. If one ordered the arjun to be cut down, the other happily provided the transport to carry it away.

Hai! The tree couldn't be saved. It was the only surviving relic of the Bandihi jungles from the Zamindari era. It still evoked memories of the past in the minds of Ketu and his friends.

When the jungles were not jungles in name only, the Shabars had been forest-dwellers. Gone were those days when they scampered off like rabbits into its dark depths the moment they heard or saw a stranger approaching. Was that why they had been identified as Khedia Shabars, in the census records?

The elders of the tribe still revered the arjun tree. They believed that it was a manifestation of the divine. Now Ketu was to be responsible for its death!

"Yes, babu. I'll cut it down," Ketu Shabar said. He stretched out his hand for ten rupees.

What a strange evening this was. He was even given what he had asked for.

"Go, go drink," Mahato said. "You won't be able to manage the job on your own, so get all those just released from jail. I'll see to it that you are all taken care of."

Ram Haldar's business did not stop with one or two trees. First, he put up posters, "Save the Forests," then, vandalized the jungles. Hands that wielded the axe were rewarded with torches, wrist watches, gleaming radios, cassette players, cycles, and of course, unlimited quantities of liquor. Each according to his capacity and capability. But the fallout was that whether innocent or guilty, the Shabars were repeatedly persecuted by the Forest Department or the Police.

Mahato's offer was much more promising. Who else would offer them so much?

"Very well, I'm going to the town now. For a meeting ... I must get some posters. How on earth can one conduct a campaign without walls? "

"Get some for me too, babu."

"Why, do you have a wall to stick them on?"

"No, no, babu. I'll spread them out on the floor when I sleep. Then I won't feel the cold in my bones."

Khedia s and Shabars are two distinct tribes in West Bengal. But in the census records they have been classified as one. "Khedia" means "runaway" in one of the dialects of West Bengal.

"All right, all right. See that you cut down the tree in two or three days. I'll have it removed when I return."

"The arjun tree, babu?"

"Yes, yes, that one. Of course, it will be like the death of a mahapatra, a noble soul ...," the monkey-capped, sweater-clad Mahato muttered as he disappeared into the foggy darkness of the night.

❦

Ketu was deep in thought. He went to look for his friends – Banamali, Diga and Pitambar – to see if they could offer a solution.

Since he was carrying liquor, they welcomed him warmly. All of them had wielded the axe. All of them were just out of jail. He who wields the axe goes to jail – that was the rule of the land. Just as it was understood that Ram Haldar would get palatial mansions built in Purulia and Bankura. That was fate. So what could they possibly do to change the order of things?

"Let me think," said Diga. Among them, Diga was treated with a little more respect. He had actually attended four whole days at the non-formal education centre! And learnt the alphabet too.

The four Shabars drowned themselves in thought and liquor. During festivals and weddings, they went around the arjun tree, beating their dhol-dhamsas. After a certain wish had been granted, the tribals made the ritual sacrifice of their hair and buried it under the tree for good luck. Hadn't Diga's father said that the tree had medicinal properties?

Drunkenly, Pitambar exclaimed, "Even the Santhals come here during the Badhna Jagoràn for the cow dance."

What a predicament! Cut the tree, you go to jail; don't cut the tree, you still get jailed. What is the Shabar to do? This prosperous village of Bandihi sits where once the jungle used to be. Now it falls under the jurisdiction of the Forest Department. But of course the Shabars don't have any claim to it.

After much contemplation, Diga said, "So why should we alone take the blame? Why should only Shabars get trapped in a false case? I'm going to tell the others. After all, they too revere the arjun. What do you say?"

Who knows how long the arjun had stood at that intersection. No one had really noticed it all these years. It was as if the tree had been there from time immemorial and would be there for time eternal. But now, all of a sudden it had become enormously important for everyone. As if it was a symbol of their existence!

The Forest Department did not control only the jungles, but the fallow land too. So where could the Shabars go? They had simply begun to wander from place to place. Wherever they saw a green patch of jungle land, they would settle down. Then the jungles would start disappearing. The fallow land would be sold off. Once again the Shabars would be homeless.

When the arjun had been a young tree, the Shabars had offered prayers to it before going on hunting expeditions. Now that it was mature, how grand it was! A shiny bark, the top touching the sky. On full-moon nights, the tree and moonlight seemed like one. During Chaitra and Baishakh, its spread of leaves provided such shade. It meant so much to them. That arjun at the crossing ...

Pitambar asked, “For how long has the arjun been guarding us? That one tree is the entire jungle for us. And our few families, the children of the forest. Now Mahato wants that very tree?”

“What can we do? Everything belongs to Bishal babu and Ram babu.”

“Till we had built our huts, we lived under the arjun. Only later did Mahato give us the land to build our huts ...” went on Pitambar.

Diga put in his bit, “Didn’t the Santhals come to it for shelter and consolation after Haldar had burnt their shanties?”

One by one, they began to recall stories about the arjun tree. Each one realized that their lives and fate were inextricably linked with that of the arjun. Society and the system had continually persecuted, exploited and almost obliterated this handful of tribals from the face of the earth. Now the same fate awaited the arjun tree, the last mute symbol of their existence.

“Bishal babu is going to town. We must collect the cash from him before he leaves,” said Diga.

“You will cut the tree then?”

"Five people should be enough to do the job. We'll ask for one hundred rupees, what do you say?"

"You may have to go to jail."

Frequent visits to the jail and constant exploitation by society had taught the Shabars to mask their true feelings and intentions. One face was presented to the Mahatos of the world, while the other one remained hidden. In the days of the British, the Shabars were the only ones who could be relied upon to set police stations and checkposts on fire. Today the babus were dependent on them, for these same Shabars performed the all-important tasks of land encroachment, crop theft, disposal of corpses and clearing government-owned forests.

So who would be so dumb as to go to jail for cutting one single tree?

Diga gave a shrewd, cunning laugh. "You don't worry about it," he told the others. After all, he knew the alphabet, had been to the jails of districts as far apart as Jamshedpur, Chaibasa, Medinipur and Bankura.

Bishal babu was assured that by the time he returned from the town, the job would be done. "Go and conduct your election meetings with an easy mind. Give us the money. When you come back, you'll see that the tree is not there. "

"Make sure that Ram babu doesn't get a hint of what is happening."

"Why, isn't he giving you the truck?"

" Yes, but he'll still create a big fuss. Also, take care that no one outside the district gets news of it."

"We'll see, babu."

On the surface, politicians hoisted different flags, but underneath, they were like sugar in milk. No conflict of interest when it came down to brass tacks.

Bishal babu, you have taught the foolish Shabars many a lesson, haven't you – what they call non-formal education!

The leaders of the two opposite camps abuse each other in public meetings. The cadre members do not understand all this. Abuses, petty quarrels and occasional bloodshed are all part of the political system. There is bound to be some dispute over the arjun too. But then, how many people would really support Ram Haldar? The entire village was under Bishal Mahato's sway.

❦

A trip to the town really becomes frenzied, thought Bishal Mahato. On the way there are speeches and gatherings at the public halls and bazaars to be attended to. In the town, so many chores have to be taken care of. Get the moped light repaired, buy a new lantern, a shawl for the wife, some medicines ...

Satisfied with his trip, Bishal Mahato was returning to Bandihi. The problem of votes had been taken care of. Oh god! When would they build a proper road to the village? Nengshai, Tetka, stream after stream, and then the descent down the bamboo bridge. After that, the tortuous way through slippery paths and uneven roads.

But as he neared the village, his head reeled.

❦

Against the backdrop of the deep blue sky, the majestic arjun tree stood with its head held high – like a guardian of the village, keeping vigil from its lofty vigil post. Once upon a time, this land used to be guarded by hundreds of leafy sentinels. One by one, they have all gone, leaving no trace. Only the arjun is left now. Alone, to guard this devastated, neglected, humiliated land of his.

Unbidden, a proverb flashed through Bishal Mahato's mind, "The leaves of the arjun tree are like the tongue of man."

All around boomed the sounds of the dhol-dhamsa-damak and the strains of the nagra. An agitated Bishal Mahato rushed into the village. A huge crowd had gathered around the arjun. Its trunk was covered with aakondo garlands.

Haldar was standing at the perimeter of the crowd, holding on to his bicycle.

"What happened?" asked Mahato.

"The gram-devata has made them do it," answered Haldar.

"What? Which ill-begotten fellow says so?"

"Diga had a dream, it seems. You paid him money in the dream and instructed him to build a concrete base around the trunk. People from all the tribes – Santhal, Khedia, Shohish, Bhumij – have now gathered to make their offerings."

"To the gram-devata?"

"Yes, and the crowds have not stopped coming. There is practically a mela on. We'd thought these fellows were fools. But they have made fools of us, Mahato!"

Bishal stepped forward to taste the full flavour of his defeat.

What a stupendous crowd! Ketu was dancing away like a maniac, going round and round with his dholok.

Bishal was suddenly afraid. This tree, these people – he knew them all. He knew them very well. And yet, today they seemed like strangers.

Fear. An uncomprehending fear gripped him.

AGNIGARBHA: THE PREFACE

translated by
Rajan Chakraborty

Peasant revolts in the State of West Bengal, as well as in other parts of India, are not just a contemporary phenomenon. The nature of exploitation of the landless peasantry by other classes, and the attempts to organize such revolts have remained the same through the ages. From the days of the Sanyasi and the Wahabi movements, and the Neel uprising, down to the modern-day Naxalbari struggle, these revolts have lent credence to people's demand for their fundamental rights.

We can analyze these revolts against the backdrop of the Naxalbari movement of May-June 1967. The population of the various districts of Darjeeling – Naxalbari, Kharibari, Fashideya – consist of about five lakh landless tribal peasants. Amongst them, are members of the Lepcha, Bhutia, Santhal, Oraon, Rajvanshi, Medi and Gorkha communities. Through the ages, these people have been exploited by the local landowners.

The longstanding Adhiar system is so designed that the big landowners advance seeds, bullocks and ploughs, fertilizers and paltry sums of money to the peasants. In return, they claim the lion's share of the harvest. Also, those with larger holdings deprive small peasants of their land on some pretext or other. This challenges man's almost primitive instinct for possession of land and provokes reaction. Thus the peasants have been consistently agitating against exploitation and oppression.

Such agitations compelled the government to pass the Estate Acquisition Act in 1954, which would prohibit an individual from possessing more than twenty-five acres of land. While the intention behind this Act cannot be doubted, in practice, it hardly affected the affluent landowners. For them, the loss of land was marginal. Most of it remained with them through "benami" transactions. Even the subsequent amendment in 1971 did not benefit the landless peasants to any great extent. It is well-known that the law is silent about the acquisition of land in the name of aqua-culture, tea plantations or industries.

The chief grievance of the Naxalbari movement was against the owners of the tea plantations. Successive generations of labourers had settled down on the plantations, and had become local residents. But they remained no more than chattels of the plantation owners. An article in the *The Statesman*, June 6, 1967, referred to the life of these labourers as "almost a state of cruel slavery." What irked the workers was the fact that the plantation owners had distributed the land, which was in excess of the permissible limit, among their loyal

---

Agnigarbha was first published in Bangla, as a collection of short stories, by Karuna Prakashani,Calcutta, 1978. The preface was translated into English especially for this volume.

retainers. Initially, the government considered taking over all such land, but the proposal was later dropped.

In the mid-50s, the Adhiars of this region launched their agitation against the tea plantation owners. They demanded that the excess land should be taken over by the government and then distributed among the landless labourers. In 1959, this agitation turned violent. As a result, the tea estate owners forcibly evicted the Adhiars from their lands and set herds of elephants loose among their dwellings.

The peasants of the Naxalbari region rose in armed rebellion, which in turn inspired revolts from the similarly exploited peasantry in Andhra Pradesh, Kerala, Tamil Nadu, Orissa and Bihar. The Congress might have celebrated a jubiliant victory in Andhra Pradesh. That does not, in any way, mean that the peasantry there was not oppressed by a regime which had let loose a reign of terror – ostensibly to curb Naxal militancy.

What is popularly known as the Naxalbari revolt has been given many names. Most people have dismissed it as a movement incited by the extreme Left, the intellectuals and frustrated youth. But whatever they may say, certain facts cannot be ignored. Nor can the signs of the revolt be wished away by saying that it happened because these groups had introduced the politics of violence into the hitherto non-violent rural India. How this problem was tackled is something everybody knows.

Rural India looks increasingly like a cremation ghat. During the summer, and in times of drought, tribals and the so-called lower-caste Hindus desperately dig up dry riverbeds in search of drinking water. The tribals of Palamau often do not get anything to eat other than the seeds of China grass. The exploitation of poor, hungry, destitute peasants continues unabated. Almost all cultivable land in the country has been cornered by a few thousand rich zamindars. Also, the landless peasants are being forced to pay exorbitant sums as compound interest on small amounts that may have been borrowed generations earlier.

The problems which had initially triggered the Naxal movement exist even today. But on this ocassion, it was seen that despite the confusion regarding the nature of the revolt, the revolt itself was crushed with considerable expertise. The fire might have raged only for a brief while but the reason why it had been started is something everyone chooses to ignore. Can the truth be denied merely because the administration chose to remain silent?

❦

The events and the context of the Naxalbari movement have been mentioned here primarily to explain the background of my stories. It cannot be denied that this was the most inspirational event of the past few decades. While no movement, either in terms of ideology or in terms of its evolution, is the ultimate truth, its true value can only be judged in posterity. And that is why the revolutionary always breaks away from the traditional path, dreams about a new world and pledges to create it.

But the problem everywhere is not necessarily about land. As a labourer working on land, the peasant is denied what is rightfully his. For him, it is a never-ending battle for water, seed and fertilizer. He lives in the midst of starvation and poverty. No middle-level cultivator has gained from the economic prosperity of the post-Independence period. However, the rich have become richer and a self-satisfied, illiterate, uncivilized affluent class has emerged. The ordinary middle class has become poorer after losing its few possessions and the lower middle class today is facing extinction. The small farmer has sold whatever he had to the zamindar, and now stands in the long line of landless peasants.

While even the basic right to live has been denied to the rural poor, the urban elite are busy in self-indulgence. When Rome burnt, Nero fiddled. Perhaps, Nero did not want to acknowledge the reasons why Rome was burning and preferred to hear the music of his fiddle. But Nero too was engulfed by the flames.

Bangla literature, for quite some time now, has indulged in this kind of escapism. Writers refuse to see the writing on the wall. What can be stranger than the fact that the writers of this country are not inspired by the diversity of its problems, cultures and customs! This extreme indifference is possible only in a country like India – semi-colonized, semi-secular and used to foreign exploitation.

Life in urban India is not much better than that in rural India either. The middle classes are losing their balance amidst increasing unemployment, skyhigh inflation, and an indifferent academic environment. The stage has been set for a class struggle. At this critical juncture every responsible writer has to take up the cause of the oppressed and the downtrodden. Otherwise history will not forgive her.

This explains why I write. It would be pointless to look for a definite political ideology in my writing. People who are sympathetic to the oppressed form the central characters in my work. The honest and conscientious teacher in my story "Jal" is a Congressman. The peasant revolt in "MW Bonam Lokhind" is the CPI Peasant Union leadership's revolt. Kali Satra, a character in "Operation Boshai Tudu" is a CPI(M) card-holder and Boshai Tudu leaves even the Naxal movement behind. The heroine of "Draupadi" is a tribal Naxal worker. They all have something in common and this similarity, according to me, is not a contradiction.

Life is not arithmetic, and human beings are not made for the game of politics. For me, all political programmes and creeds should aim at the realization of the claims of human beings to survival and justice. I desire a transformation of the present social system. I do not believe in narrow party politics.

Thirty-one years after the Independence, I am yet to see the people of this country overcome shortages of food and drinking water. A pure, unadulterated anger against a system that has not been able to uplift these people, is the only inspiration for all my writings. It is my belief that both the Leftist and Rightist parties have failed to fulfil the promises they made to the electorate. I do not think this situation will change in my lifetime.

So I go on writing ... To the best of my ability ... All my life I have written about people so that I should not be ashamed of facing myself. Because a writer is judged in her lifetime itself, and it becomes her responsibility to explain herself.

The Crafting Years

1926	Born on January 14, in Dhaka.
1944	She works for the People's Relief Committee during the Bengal Famine.
1946	She graduates in English literature from Vishwabharati.
1947	She marries Bijon Bhattacharya, the eminent playwright.
1948	Nabarun, her son, is born on June 23.
1949	She works as a teacher at the Ramesh Mitra Institution.
1950	The Post and Telegraph Department employs her as an upper division clerk.
1956	*Jhansir Rani*, her first historical biography, is published.
1957	*Nati*, her first novel, appears in print.
1958	Her first collection of stories, *Ki Basante Ki Sarate,* is released.
1961	She gets a divorce from Bijon Bhattacharya.
1963	She finishes her master's in English from Calcutta University – seventeen years after her BA.
1964	She joins Bijayagarh Jyotish Roy College as a lecturer and teaches there till 1984.
1965	She marries Asit Gupta.
1968	The Amrita Puraskar is awarded to her.
1976	She goes through a second divorce.
1978	She is honoured with the Saratchandra Chattopadhyay Memorial Medal.
1979	She receives the Sahitya Akademi Award for her novel *Aranyer Adhikar.*
1980	She starts *Bartika*, a Bangla quarterly devoted to socio-political and tribal issues. The Palamau Jila Bonded Labour Liberation Oraganization is founded by her.
1981	She receives a medal from the Nikhil Bharat Banga Sahitya Sammelan.
1982	She is with the Bangla daily *Jugantar* as a reporter.

1983 Calcutta University honours her with the Bhuvanmohini Medal. She is the president of the Harijan Workers Union of Beharampur Municipality.

1984 She is made the president of the West Bengal Khedia Shabar Kalyan Samiti.

1985 She is in Paris as part of an Indo-French cultural exchange programme.

1986 The Padma Shri is conferred on her. One of the Indian delegates at the Frankfurt Book Fair, she also travels in West Germany and England on a lecture tour.

1988 She visits the USA on the invitation of the Marxist Study Circle of Pittsburgh University.

1989 Calcutta University awards her the prestigious Jagattarini Gold Medal.

1990 She visits eight American universities as a Fulbright lecturer.

1992 She represents India at a summit on "Economic Advancement of Rural Women in the Third World," held in Geneva.

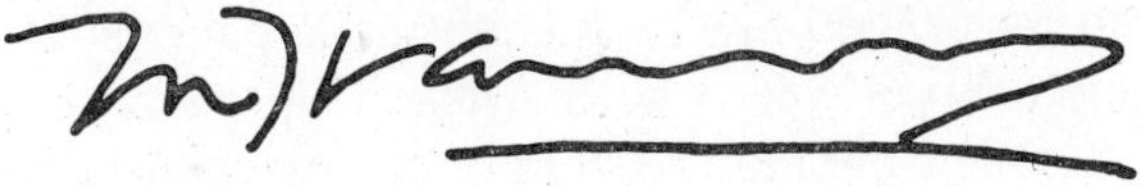

M T VASUDEVAN NAIR

"When he smokes beedis, so do some of his readers. Even superstar Mammootty smokes beedis, it is said, because MT does so."

– M Mukundan

MT VasudevanNair. Cult figure extraordinaire. The script-writer with the golden touch, a charismatic director. Mentor to a whole generation of writers in Malayalam. The most popular living writer in Kerala. Now the recipient of the Jnanpith Award, India's highest literary honour.

MT to most people, accolades and adulation have never been lacking for this writer-cum-editor-cum-filmmaker. His work has fetched him awards from the Kerala Sahitya Akademi (in 1959, 1978 and 1981) and the Sahitya Akademi (1970). He has also received the Vayalar Award (1984), the Katha Award for Creative Fiction

(1992) and the Otakhuzal Award (1993). An immensely successful scriptwriter and director, his debut venture, *Nirmalyam*, won the National Award for Best Film and the President's Gold Medal (1973). *Kadavu*, his most recent directorial effort, received awards at the Singapore International Film Festival and the Tokyo International Telefilm Festival. Some of his screenplays too have been honoured with national and state awards.

The youngest of four children, MT was born on July 15, 1933, in the quiet village of Kudallur in central Kerala. His father was a farmer. The 1940s, that saw socio-political upheavals in many parts of the country, somhow by-passed this little village that sat on the banks of the rippling Bharathapuzha. "He was an introvert, a sensitive boy," recalls his cousin, Kathyayani Amma. "An incurable book-lover, he once wrote the whole of Changampuzha's *Ramanam* in his note-book as the copy was not available. When he was in the eighth class, Vasu wrote a drama, *Sivaji Athava Katteli*, but hid it behind a big box."

Such idyllic times don't last forever. Disaster destroyed the quiet contentment of Kudallar as cholera, famine and the cyclone played havoc with the little village. MT was witness to a misery and suffering he could never have imagined existed. This experience was the forge in which his mind as a writer was honed and sharpened, etching scenes and characters into an eternal part of his self, informing all that poured forth from his seething imagination from that moment on.

In 1953, MT, then a Chemistry undergraduate of twenty, entered the *Mathrubhumi* International Short Story Contest and won the first prize. This paved the way for other short and long fiction, each one of them startlingly fresh in approach and outlook, each one setting new standards for this seemingly tireless iconoclast. His first collection of stories, *Raktham Puranda Mantharikal* (The Blood-Stained Sand), was published even before he had graduated from

---

This quote is from an interview with M Mukundan, Malayalam novelist, in *The Times of India*, January 28, 1996.

Victoria College in Palghat. And in 1954, he won the Kerala Sahitya Akademi Award for his first novel *Naluketttu*. Based on the breaking down of the old matriarchal society of Kerala, the novel took the Malayalam-reading world by storm.

After a brief stint as a school teacher, MT joined the *Mathrubhumi* group as an editorial assistant. He gave up his job in 1981, only to return to the same group in 1989. He is now the Chief Editor of all its periodicals.

MT is considered to be largely responsible for the resurgence of short fiction in Malayalam. He appeared on the Malayalam literary scene when it was dominated by the Socialist Realists, whose works spewed fire and fury. Into this landscape, MT brought in the gentle breeze from the Malabar coast, the greenery of his sylvan village, Kudallur, and the sparkling freshness of the river Nila. Woven into the fabric of this pastoral idyll are memories of misery and destruction wrought in the village of his childhood. It is these vignettes of suffering that influenced MT's quintessential modernist vision – a vision that blends inner and outer landscapes, that lays bare the conflict between traditional family values in a decadent and decaying feudalistic social structure and the progressive, but increasingly materialistic, modern economy.

His literary output consists of nearly twenty anthologies of short stories, eight novels, forty-seven screenplays, five collections of essays, two travelogues and a play. He has also written two books for children *Manikya Kallu* (1957) and *Daya, Enna Penkutty* (1987). *Manikya Kallu* is presently being filmed by an Indo-American film company.

MT has served as Director of the Film Finance Corporation and as a guest lecturer at the Pune Film Institute. He is now the President of the Kerala Sahitya Akademi and the Chairperson of the Thunjan Smaraka Samiti. He lives in Khozikode with his wife, Kalamandalam Saraswati, and two daughters.

Self-confessedly, MT is a craftsman rather than an innovator; meticulously fashioning each and every word to a flawless perfection. A couple of stories a year, a novel in five or six year's time, is all that he allows himself to pen. He says, "I reject a lot in my mind before setting anything down on paper."

Apart from his own immensely valuable corpus of work, MT has contributed to the growth of literature in Malayalam by identifying and nurturing many new and exciting talents over the years. As the editor of the *Mathrubhumi* periodicals, he takes an avid interest in the literary happenings in and outside Kerala. Gifted writers like M Mukundan and Paul Zacharia were first noticed by him. And such is his mesmeric hold over the writing community that, unlike many other successful writers, he inspires awe, not envy, admiration and an intense desire to emulate, not jealousy. Such feelings can only augur excellence for Indian literature.

M T VASUDEVAN NAIR

in conversation with
Vanajam Ravindran

On November 24, 1995 I met MT in his Mathrubhumi *office. The smell of tobacco pervaded the book-lined room strewn with newspapers and magazines. Though he strikes one as being rather reticent and aloof, MT became animated when speaking of his childhood, his obsession with creative writing, and his despair at the drying up of Bharatapuzha on the banks of which he grew up. In the course of the interview one caught a glimpse of another aspect of this silent man – an inborn humility unaffected by steady success.*

***VR:** MT, of all the career options open to you, why did you choose to be a fiction writer?*

MT: When I was young, Vaikom Muhammad Basheer, Thakazhi Sivasankara and Karur Nilakanta Pillai, were established writers in Malayalam. They were my idols. I used to read their stories, and everything else that came into my hands. If somebody had asked me – a young village boy – what I would like to be when I grew up, I would have said, A writer, like all these great people!

I was born and brought up in a village beyond the hills. The nearest railway station was six miles away; the high school was six miles away. I would go to school every morning and return in the evening, walking over the hills.

Getting a magazine or a book to read was difficult. I used to borrow books from here and there, and sometimes I would come across a special issue of some magazine which had photographs of the great writers. In fact I had cut out pictures of Changambuzha, Karur, Kesav Dev, Varki, Thakazhi and Basheer and pasted them on the walls of my room.

> IF SOMEBODY HAD ASKED ME – A VILLAGE BOY – WHAT I WOULD LIKE TO BE WHEN I GREW UP, I WOULD HAVE SAID, A WRITER!

When I was eleven or twelve, I started writing poems. After a while I turned to short stories. At times I tried writing essays too. All I knew was that I wanted to be a writer. And I went on writing – experimenting, dabbling in all forms. When I was fourteen, during my holidays, I wrote a poem practically every day, a short story once in two or three days, and sent them to some magazine.

***VR:** You have always spoken against imitating someone else's style. Have you been consciously trying to write against an existing style or styles?*

MT: If you ask me whom I admired most in those days, I would say S K Pottekkat and Basheer. But I never thought I would be able to write like either of them. I started with the idea of writing poetry, short stories and essays. Much later, say at 15 or 16, I don't know how, I came to the decision that the short story was the most suitable form for me. Then I gave up writing poetry and essays, believing it was best to stick to one form.

You can't develop a style all of a sudden. You go on writing. You know it's not quite right yet. After trying repeatedly, you evolve a style of your own. It takes many, years. I must have developed mine in my late fifties – when I was 55 or 56. But till then, you are like an amateur, experimenting with style.

***VR:** Was your family supportive in your initial attempts to write?*

MT: No. We were basically an agricultural family. My mother had not had any conventional schooling. She had probably studied under the nattezuthachans, the village gurus. But she was interested in myths and things like that. My father was away in Ceylon. So I didn't have any contact with him at that time. Although we did not have a literary background, all my brothers – I was the youngest of four children – got books from wherever they could. In that sense we had a congenial atmosphere at home. But nobody really encouraged me to write. In fact, much later, when my father came back from Ceylon he said, "This chap is ruining his life. He doesn't have a career. He's always sitting in a corner and scribbling away. He is a good-for-nothing fellow." But my teachers and the older writers in the locality – they sort of encouraged me.

***VR:** Would you say something about your actual writing habits – is it all planned out well in advance or do you write in fits and starts?*

MT: As far as short stories are concerned, when something strikes a chord within me, I play with the idea for a long time. I let it take shape in my mind. Only then do I begin to write. This is not possible with novels. You begin with a rough idea, a vague outline. But with the short story I am very definite. I go on thinking about the idea, brooding over it. Until it evolves into its final form.

***VR:** What do you think of short fiction as a genre? Do all short stories have the potential for being developed into novels? Which do you think is your forte – the short story or the novel?*

MT: I have a partiality for the short story. For one thing, it is not so elaborate. Something strikes you – and at that instant, you know there is the germ of a story in it. You think about it. When it is almost mature in your mind, you live with it for one or two days. And then you are into it. But novels require a lot of planning. Besides, there is the time factor.

In a short story you can almost achieve perfection. Structurally, it is closer to a poem. A lot of compact emotions can go into it. You go on chiselling it, removing unwanted portions till you finally get the exact form. A good short story means that when you get its final form you can't replace a word or a sentence with another. You can get that kind of perfection in the short story. It is a powerful literary form. It can be like a laugh or a cry from your heart – deep and intense. Whereas in a novel, perfection is impossible. Even when I go through a finished novel, I feel certain portions are weak, that I could have done better.

As to whether every short story is a potential novel – no. Only after I make sure that there isn't sufficient material for a novel do I write a short story. I don't want to stretch a short story and make it into a novel. I am not concerned about the length of my writings, they may be six or sixty pages long. Some of my short stories, "Vanaprastham" for example, are very long.

YOU CAN'T DEVELOP A STYLE ALL OF A SUDDEN. I MUST HAVE DEVELOPED MINE WHEN I WAS 55 OR 56.

***VR:** Why do you write – because of a compulsive urge to prove something or is it to get something off your chest?*

MT: In the beginning I wanted to declare to all the world – Here I am, a village boy sitting in his room and writing. I was obsessed with the act of writing. But much later I realized that obsession alone would not do, that writing should achieve a magic of its own. Only when the two combine can your work be good. As for getting something off my chest – yes, there are certain short stories, certain novels which do weigh on me. There is no escape till you write them down. Or else they haunt you, go on disturbing you. But it is not always like that.

VR: *In your significant writings, whether fiction or screenplays – in "Bandhanam,"* Asuravithu, Nalukettu *and* Nirmalyam *for instance – certain themes recur: the dying social and cultural institutions of the Nair community, and the dichotomy between the city and the village. Are these informed by a conscious social message or are they perhaps the unconscious expressions of a romantic strain in you?*

MT: There is no conscious social message in my work. A writer is moulded by the set-up in which he grows up. I was born in a Nair joint family in a matrilineal social order. There was a lot of raw material that a writer could draw upon in that set-up. Later I used the same material for my screenplays too. As a writer I am most concerned about the human situation and for me this is linked with the joint family and with village life.

VR: *A related question – M N Karasseri has remarked that the city is the chief villain in your fictional universe. But, the characters in your fiction, seem to need that exposure for their personal growth. Do you see this as a contradiction or is the death of innocence a necessary evil?*

MT: What Karasseri said is true. In a number of my works it is the city that corrupts. But in my latest short story, *Silanikhitam*, published two months back, I have shown the village in an uncomplimentary light. The village is not always innocent. It has the potential for evil too.

The death of innocence is a universal problem. It is the refrain of many of our Kerala writers. The fortunate ones have had three levels of experience. They were born in a village, they had to go to college in a small town and later they reached a big city. As for me, I have two levels of experience – the village and the small town. The death of innocence is a favourite theme of mine. You realize the value of innocence only when you lose it.

VR: *To what extent are your stories autobiographical?*

MT: There will always be a few personal experiences here and there in my writings. But that is true of most fiction writers. Bits and pieces of their lives will go into the making of a work. But I will not say that this work is autobiographical and the other is not so, and so on. Many people think Appunni of *Nalukettu* is an extension of my self. He is not. He is just another boy who witnesses the problems of a matrilineal family. But Setu of *Kalam* is a lot like me. I share with Setu his emotional experiences and the situations he has been through.

VR: *MT, though you belong to a region bristling with political activities, you are comparatively uninvolved in politics. Would you describe yourself as an apolitical writer?*

MT: Many people have asked me this. Yes, I grew up in a place that was alive with political activities. I was naturally interested in them but I did not use them as raw material for my writing. And I don't know why. I have written about the social implications of political events. But politics as such does not interest me – no, not even now.

AS A WRITER I AM MOST CONCERNED ABOUT THE HUMAN SITUATION AND THIS IS LINKED WITH THE JOINT FAMILY AND WITH VILLAGE LIFE.

VR: *And yet your notion of history demands attention. In the short story, "Sukritam," you make the impersonal narrator say:* We are the historians and the history. *In* Randamoozham (The Second in Line)*, the subversive anti-epic, the events of the Mahabharata are seen through Bhima's eyes. This implies an engagement with historical interpretation. Would you elaborate on this?*

MT: The *Mahabharata* has always fascinated me. I grew up listening to its stories. But later, when I read and reread it, something struck me. The second brother Bhima, who has won all the battles, is not considered a hero; he is sidelined. There is one incident in Vyasa's *Mahabharata* in which Arjuna's son, Abhimanyu, dies fighting a great battle. There is much lamentation. Later, Bhima's son, Ghatotkacha, dies and, with eyes streaming with tears, Yudhishtira says that he was the first born among the grandsons of the Pandavas. Lord Krishna, who appears then, asks the weeping multitude, "Why do you lament? You should rejoice over his death. After all he was a rakshasa." Bhima stands close by, listening to Krishna's words. Actually this scene was the beginning of *Randamoozham*. Thereafter I started reading the whole epic from this perspective. I went forwards and backwards and finally came to the conclusion that the actual history of the war is ignored in the epic. I wanted to rework it. I may not be overtly "political," but I am conscious of what is happening around me. The problem is that one's perspective is more often than not shaped and manipulated by extraneous factors. I don't want to fall into that trap.

***VR:** You are an avid reader of Western fiction. Has it influenced your use of certain narrative techniques?*

MT: No. I started reading Western fiction during my college days. All that reading has helped me in one sense – it has made me aware of the possibilities of fiction, of the ample scope for freedom in the sense that there are no hard and fast rules. I have not directly borrowed any narrative technique from Western fiction. But it stimulated me to keep searching for a form of my own.

***VR:** MT, your creative output has been steady and quite formidable. Does it mean that you have never experienced what is called the writer's block?*

MT: Actually I have not written all that much. But I do maintain a steady flow of writing. Of course, between 1976 and '78, I was quite ill and after that I was rather hesitant to write. To overcome that, I first wrote a few articles and then resumed fiction writing. To my pleasant surprise there was no problem – no writer's block at all.

VR: *Could you say something about the most exciting moments of your creative experience?*

MT: You see, each time you begin to write something, each time you successfully finish it, you feel thrilled. For instance, I had done a lot of painstaking reading, taken down elaborate notes for *Randamoozham* And I finished the first draft in 27 days. I was working 12-14 hours a day. When the first draft was finished I felt excited. Of course, I worked for more than 60 days on the second draft. But the finishing of the first draft, whether it's a novel or a short story, is a great moment.

VR: *What kind of a reader did you have in mind, when you started writing? Do you think of a reading audience beyond the regional frontier ?*

MT: No, when I am working on something, I am not bothered by the thought of a prospective readership or the reader response. Only when I get the feedback from total strangers do I become aware of the reaction to my stories. I am not concerned as to whether a Malayali reader will appreciate my work or whether in translation it will reach beyond the frontiers of Kerala. These are incidental. While working I am totally engrossed in the work. It is a struggle with words – a struggle with the raw material – to conquer it to give it a form. The next struggle is while publishing it – wondering whether it will reach people.

THE FINISHING OF THE FIRST DRAFT, WHETHER IT'S A NOVEL OR A SHORT STORY, IS A GREAT MOMENT.

VR: *This takes us to the realm of translation. You have translated into Malayalam, the English rendering of some Russian stories.*

MT: I have translated very little – a few Russian stories and some French. I enjoyed doing it because I was introducing writers like Dostoevsky to Malayalam readers. But they are difficult to translate and I don't have the time for translation now.

VR: *Are you generally satisfied with the translations of your stories?*

MT: I have read some of the translations. See, it's very difficult to get the regional flavour in translation. But at the same time it should be readable and appealing to a non-Malayali. I discussed this matter with a translator once, who had retained a certain word – asaripparambu. I felt that though regional flavour may be lost, the story would be clearer if he had used its equivalent in English, "the carpenter's house." Some of the translations of my short stories are good. But I don't think any author would be fully satisfied with a translation.

VR: *As the Chief Editor of* Mathrubhumi, *you're a practising critic yourself. Is the critic in you constantly breathing down your neck when you write fiction?*

MT: Before I sit down to write fiction (and that's why I write very little these days – I have written only two short stories in the last six months), I always ask myself – Is it necessary to write this? If I get a sure answer – Yes, there's no harm in attempting it, such and such levels of experience can be brought out – I begin to write. What I ask myself is whether I am repeating something. I reject a lot of possibilities before setting down anything on paper.

VR: *A critic recently said that modern Malayalam writers tend to move away from readers because their theme and content, borrowed from the West, are incomprehensible to them. How do you react to this view?*

MT: I don't think they are either borrowing themes from the West or moving away from the readers. These writers have a discriminating readership. These readers don't approach books for momentary enjoyment. They expect something serious from the authors. These writers may be familiar with Western techniques and craft, but they have their individual styles.

VR: *What is your attitude to feminist fiction in Malayalam?*

MT: In Kerala we have had women writers all along. For instance, just as we evaluate the period of Thakazhi and Kesav Dev, we will be considering that of Lalithambika Antharjanam too. There has been no distinction between men and women writers in Malayalam. It is only recently that we have started talking of feminist writing. The work of K Saraswathi Amma has now been classified as "feminist."

VR: What about writers like Kamala Das, Sarah Joseph?

MT: They are excellent writers. Why should we label them? There is no harm in classifying them, but I feel they belong to the mainstream of fiction writers.

***VR:** Do you subscribe to the current or not so current Barthean notion of "the death of the author?"*

MT: I have heard of the theory but have not really studied it. Of course, as a writer I have certain definite views regarding this. When I am writing I know that I am not important, I am only instrumental. Somehow the words come to me. And what I write may not reach the reader as such. The reader always adds some personal experience and creates a new story in his/her mind. I have always believed this. Suppose I write a story and it ends there, there is no meaning in it. The story actually begins after the reader has finished reading it and something else is grafted on to it. Thus my novel becomes another novel in the process of being read by someone; my short story becomes another short story. To this extent I agree with the idea of the death of the author.

BEFORE I SIT DOWN TO WRITE FICTION, I ALWAYS ASK MYSELF – IS IT NECESSARY TO WRITE THIS?

***VR:** In that case would you allow the translator the same kind of freedom to interpret a writer's work?*

MT: Yes. If the translator follows exactly the syntax and diction of the original, the meaning might not be clear in the target language. The translator, by exercising a certain freedom, helps the text to reach a different set of readers.

VR: *How would you, as a creative writer, like your work to be interpreted? Are you generally wary of academic criticism?*

MT: When I read some of the interpretations, I am surprised. I feel here's an element I have not seen myself. When the critic says a text has this dimension or that, she is using the material to be creative. To that extent I admire her. As for my reactions to criticism – favourable or otherwise – I have to take it in my stride as long as I am in this line. When someone praises me I am not unduly happy. Similarly when the criticism is unfavourable I feel the critic has the right to condemn a book.

VR: *Would you say the confrontation between creative literature and the modern mass media augurs ill for the former?*

MT: The writer has to survive in an era which is dominated by mass media and the electronic media. So, if you want your voice to be heard in this chaos, there is a problem. But I am not worried. The written word has its own importance and faithful following. Whatever may be the challenges from the world of technology, the written word, the book will survive.

VR: *So you don't subscribe to the view that readership is generally dwindling in Kerala.*

MT: I don't know. But the younger generation here doesn't learn Malayalam any more. That is partly because of the educational system. Most children go to English medium schools and after the fifth or sixth standard study only English and Hindi. But all said and done, publishers say that their books are selling well – at least the books of major writers. Certainly readership will decrease when all the youngsters who come out of college are ignorant of Malayalam. But then again, when I look back to my student days, I realize that both in school and college very few boys used to read books, whether in Malayalam or in English. The prospect is not so bleak therefore.

VR: *Has your passionate involvement in film making been an impediment to writing in any way?*

MT: I consider myself a writer who occasionally intrudes into films. Once in two or three years I make a film or write a script. Films are not my full-time occupation. I keep the two areas separate – films on one side and literature, my main interest, on the other.

VR: *To me, "Sukritam" seems to have immense cinematic potential. Are you thinking of filming it?*

MT: Yes, it depicts how myths are created in a society. Yes, I will think about making it into a film.

VR: *Talking of films,* Nirmalyam *is an incomparably brilliant one. Would you say something about screenplay writing?*

MT: The screenplay is the blueprint of a film and the director, its architect. Literature is one of the six or seven arts that go into the making of a film. The screenplay is half technical and half literary. Of course some of the best screenplays, for instance Ingmar Bergman's, read like excellent literature. Of course, without the spoken word Bergman can portray an emotion eloquently. But sometimes the spoken word has its own role to play. In the French classic, *The Wages of Fear,* these down and out drivers are carrying liquid dynamite to a mine in flames. On the way a middle aged man asks a young man, "What's your age?" He replies, "I feel 100." This emotion could have been conveyed with just acting talent or the filming. But the words, "I feel 100," speak volumes.

THE TRANSLATOR, BY EXERCISING A CERTAIN FREEDOM, HELPS THE TEXT TO REACH A DIFFERENT SET OF READERS.

VR: *You are a prolific writer, a busy editor and an involved film-maker and director. What kind of discipline do you enforce on yourself to meet the rigorous deadlines entailed in all these activities?*

MT: When I am here in office, I attend only to my journalistic responsibilities. As far as work is concerned, I have a one track mind. That is my problem. When I am writing a short story or a novel I can't attend to any other work. Or when I am editing something I can do only that. I read a little for my own survival. In between, I take a few days off. I go away to do what I really want to do. Whether writing or film-making. I do nothing else, switching off everything else.

And when I come back, it takes a while for me to reorganize. It is difficult. I know I am overworked. Which is why I cut down on film assignments. I have to make time for my first priority – writing.

VR: *What would be your advice to young writers of Malayalam, aspiring to write fiction today?*

MT: They should first know what has already been written. I always tell them that they should be bold enough to reject quite a bit of what they write, after reading and rereading it, although it is natural for young writers to get excited about every new idea that strikes them. It used to happen to me. The second thing I tell them is to be patient, to brood over the idea. Once it is written, they should reread the story after their excitement has cooled down. I tell them to read a lot by other writers; not to get direct inspiration from them but to keep their minds active, to enrich the soil into which to plant their own seeds. This kind of reading is like adding manure to that soil. However, in creative writing, no one is competent to give advice to anybody. Each has his or her own method. And one has to be prepared for rejections – first by oneself and later by the readers. And if one has the confidence, one should keep on writing.

VR: *Do you believe that a writer can influence people's attitude through his writings? For instance,* Kilivathililude *(*Glimpses through the Window*) suggests your deep anguish at the degeneration of humanity through environmental pollution and the general degradation of human society.*

MT: When I see what is happening to the Bharatapuzha, on the banks of which I grew up, reduced to a desert, dying through pollution, I feel sad and indignant. I write letters to the concerned ministers and other authorities. But nobody listens. At least when I write or speak about these problems as a writer, I have the satisfaction that I have done what little I can, although that will not bring about any change.

***VR:** Do you think it necessary to interact with other regional writers?*

MT: On a personal level, I have a lot of contact with other regional writers. It is good to know what is happening next doors. We know a lot about what is happening in Latin American literature and other foreign literatures. Yet we are so ignorant of the trends in Kannada, Marathi or Bangla writings. I like meeting writers from other parts of India.

***VR:** Which would you rate as some of your best writing?*

MT: I really can't say. When I finished "Kadugannava," my last short story, I thought it my best. But then, other works like "Sherlock" and "Sukritam" are equally my favourites. Of no story can I say that I like it the best. A lot depends on the satisfaction you feel after writing a piece and your various associations with the writing of a story.

I ALWAYS TELL [YOUNG WRITERS] THEY SHOULD BE BOLD ENOUGH TO REJECT QUITE A BIT OF WHAT THEY WRITE.

***VR:** One last question, what do you plan to write next?*

MT: I have a couple of ideas in mind. One is a long short story set in Benaras. I don't know whether it will become a novel once I start writing. I don't generally plan out the length of what I am going to write. I have already begun a novel, *Manikkinavu*. If I am free for 3-4 months I should be able to complete the first draft. At the moment I am not thinking of any film project.

SUKRITAM

translated by
Vanajam Ravindran

As the month of Karkitakam came to a close and the skies cleared, we gave up all hope of finding Cheriyatti. That was when a woman was seen trudging along the narrow path at the foot of Thani hills. With slow steps, she came into the courtyard of the Kanancheri house. Then, throwing off the tattered cloth that covered her from head to foot, she let out a heart-rending cry, a sound like the splitting of tender bamboo shoot. "Amma ..."

Atti and her four brothers rushed to the front door and stopped, speechless. There stood their dear Cheriyatti, young Cheriyatti, who had been lost in the forest. Atti trembled, overcome with joy. "Oh my daughter! You've come back at last," she exclaimed, as soon as she found her voice.

Cheriyatti's uncles recovered from the shock and ran in different directions to let the nattukoottam know of their niece's return. The people, relieved that their paradevata – their household deity – had not completely abandoned them, turned to the south and offered short fervent prayers.

❦

Our people have faced grievous dangers in the past. But those seem trivial compared with the menace that recently swept through our land with thundering hoof beats, raising clouds of dust.

The news that an invading army was coming down the pass from the North had first reached Tampuran, the ruler of our desam. At once he ordered all three of his palanquins to be prepared. He left in the first one, taking the royal ornaments and the idol of Goddess Bhagavati with him. His consorts followed in the other two palanquins. Escorted by their retinue, they were swiftly borne across the borders and over the Chammini hills to foreign lands.

Soon after, terror-stricken messengers came running from the furthest limits of the land to inform the nattukoottam of the impending danger. They talked of marauding invaders, mounted on fierce fire-spitting beasts, who were fast closing in, leaving devastation in their wake.

The leader of the nattukoottam sent out his messengers immediately. They beat their drums and ordered the people to gather their jewel boxes and the keys of their granaries and, if possible, seek refuge with their cattle in the Chundolakkala forests beyond the Thani hills. The messenger-warrior who reached us first, travelling as fast as wind, was later awarded the grand title –

"Sukritam" (A Virtuous Deed) first appeared in Malayalam in *Vanaprastham*, a recent collection of MT's short stories. This story is one of his favourites. It was first published in this translation in *Indian Literature* (Sahitya Akademi, 1995).

"Parakotti Ammaman" or "the drumbeating uncle." With time this was shortened to "Paramman" and the ritual of making offerings to him came into vogue. And then the practice of slaughtering fowls in his name, on the night of the new moon in the month of Medam, started.

As soon as the invading army entered the land, they dragged out, and sent to the gallows, the native warriors who had hidden in the banana groves and behind the haystacks. The four fields on the river bank later came to be called the "gallow fields." Seeing the dense clouds which augured the onset of the monsoons, the invaders decided to move southwards to avoid any flash floods. And we, realizing that the enemy had departed, returned to our homes.

This incident was recorded on copper plates. Years later, our children, studying the history of their native land based on these plates, were taught: The ruler of Thavinjanadu deigned to meet the Nawab. Much later this same statement was recorded by one of our research scholars who chanced upon the copper plate inscriptions preserved at Orumanassery. The fact, however, is that in those days our land was bereft of a ruler and we cannot say with certainty who the ruler referred to is. And we do not want to find out either. For *we* are the historians and the history. What we do know is that Thavinjanadu is a corruption of "the nadu (land) deserted by the Devi." But enough of this. Let us move on to the glories of our temple.

❦

The people performed the ritual cleansing of their hearths and homes, soon after they returned. The nattukoottam quickly assembled in the shade of the twin banyan trees. They had barely got the palm leaves ready on which to reckon their various losses, when young Kalia came rushing in. "Cheriyatti of the Kanancheri

---

Nattukoottam: Literally the citizenry; but in the social context of the Kerala of the 18th-19th centuries, the representatives of all important families or tarawads who virtually ruled the desam, a cluster of villages.

tarawad is not to be found," he gasped.

"Young Cheriyatti not to be found!"

The nattukoottam were shocked. Their very universe trembled!

They remembered how distressed they had been when Atti, the only sister to four brothers did not have a child to carry on the tarawad. Eager to hear the patter of little feet there, the community had made a concerted effort to invoke the deities, by providing load-rests for porters, constructing shelters along the highways to provide drinking water for tired wayfarers. Atti prayed and fasted for forty-one days. Finally, she had been blessed with a daughter. Though the baby girl was named Ittati, she was fondly called Cheriyatti – little Atti – by her mother and uncles. It was when this little child, the favourite of all the land, had blossomed into a young maiden, that the marauders passed through the area and turned it in to a wasteland.

An enquiry was conducted. Atti and the eldest woman of the community were summoned by the nattukoottam. Atti informed them that Cheriyatti had definitely been among the women and children who had gone into hiding. The girls had always stayed in groups. But one day Cheriyatti had gone for a swim in the forest spring, accompanied only by her young pinati. When the child did not return, no one had been worried. Cheriyatti had friends of her age among the other Ettuveettukar families and she often spent time with them. But she had not been with them!

"O my land! The Devi has abandoned you!" the chief of the nattukoottam let out an anguished cry.

❦

The monsoons came again. Messengers brought news that our Tampuran, who had fled from his desam, had been given land by the Perumbadappu Raja. And he was going to build a temple and install the deity there.

Ettuveettukar: The eight (ettu) illustrious tarawads.

Pinati: Women who waited upon the female members of prominent tarawads.

The monsoon ended, but the tears coursing down Atti's cheeks would not be stemmed. We were beginning to despair because both the astrologer and the singing soothsayer had not been able to get a clue to Cheriyatti's whereabouts through their divination. It was then that the young girl suddenly appeared.

The nattukoottam assembled in the Kanancheri courtyard. Atti looked at her young daughter, hiding behind a carved pillar, staring at her toe nails, absorbed in some beautiful dream. She called out to the girl, "Speak my daughter, speak. Whatever happened to you, my child? Let the menfolk hear."

When she came out after her dip in the spring and was changing her clothes, Cheriyatti recounted, the pinati had whispered that a stranger was standing behind the thickets. No sooner had the pinati said that, the stranger appeared in front of Cheriyatti – a soldier! Seeing his lecherous eyes and outstretched arms, she ran as fast as she could to save her honour, crying out, "Oh, Devi, protect me."

Inflamed by desire, the soldier followed, in hot pursuit of his prey. Hunted like a gentle deer, she fled till she fell at the feet of a stranger.

"Who? Who was he?" asked the nattukoottam in consternation.

"A hunter, a hunter from the forest."

Cheriyatti continued her story. The hunter hid her in a bower of dense creepers till her besotted pursuer gave up and went back the way he had come, sorely disappointed.

Cheriyatti lived in the hunter's hut till she was free from danger. The hunter, said Cheriyatti, had fed her honey and wild fruit and had given her a mat to sleep on. He had stood at the entrance of the hut with his spear and his bow and arrows, guarding her from wild animals and enemy soldiers.

"Tampuratti, where's my daughter? Where's the pinati, respected

---

Tampuratti: The respectful way of addressing a woman of a Nair household. The men would be addressed as Ejamanan or Tampuran.

Vanian: A person belonging to the caste whose traditional profession was extracting oil from seeds.

masters?" asked a vanian agitatedly, from where he stood, some distance away.

Atti's fourth brother was furious. How dare a vanian speak to them like this? He promptly drew his sword. If the chief of the nattukoottam had not pardoned the vanian for his thoughtless misdemeanour he might have been killed! Glad that his life had been spared, the vanian promptly withdrew from there and listened to the interrogations from afar.

The hut was at the other end of the forest, said Cheriyatti, so the news of the enemies' withdrawal had reached them much later. The hunter then took her back along the shortest and least tortuous route, she walking in front and he, behind her. When they reached the outskirts of their land, he had turned and gone back the way they had come.

Having said all this, Cheriyatti covered her lotus-like face with soft, delicate hands and sobbed and sobbed, till she slumped at the foot of the pillar, exhausted. The nattukoottam dispersed after deciding to reassemble at dusk.

❦

That night a grand feast was prepared at the Kanancheri tarawad to which the members of the other seven Ettuveettukar tarawads came.

The leaves were laid for the first batch of guests – the women and children. When food was about to be served, a venerable old grandmother asked, "Tell me, oh you, my wise brothers, is it proper to allow a girl, who has eaten food from a hunter and shared his mat, to enter the nalakaya, this inner courtyard?"

Not one of us had thought of this in the hurry and scurry of preparing the feast. Our ruler, who should have advised us on such matters, was elsewhere. So the alternative had to be Cheramballi Cherunni Ejaman, the oldest member of the community. He would be able to give us an answer to the old lady's question.

Promptly Cheriyatti's uncles and a member of the nattukoottam ran to the Cheramballi tarawad. After long and deep deliberation, Cheramballi Ejaman said, "No, my nephews, it's not proper. It is not proper."

The guests, who had come to the feast, left without even a sip of water. Overnight the news spread and scandalized women said, "Just imagine, the virgin of Kanancheri in the bed of a hunter! Oh, our paradevatas, let not evil befall our children!"

We had always conducted ourselves honourably, living in awe and fear of our virtuous and illustrious ancestors, so that our land would be protected. The karanavar of the Kanancheri tarawad knew this very well. Pacing the courtyard restlessly, he summoned his sister.

"Light the lamp upstairs," he ordered her.

Standing before the lamp the venerable old ammaman, still in his wet clothes after his ablutions, prayed fervently, invoking all his valorous ancestors – Thasammaman, Kandamman, Koppamman, cheriya Koppamman , and the rest of them. His body trembled as he touched the lighted lamp and made a vow. Then he came out, as if in a trance, and asked his sister and the younger generation of the tarawad, "Do you want the tarawad disgraced? Do you want the land ruined?"

His voice had assumed a different tone. It was as if all our ancestors were speaking through him.

Cheriyatti, lying half asleep close to the wall, woke up with a start. Standing in the doorway were her mother and her uncles. Her mother was weeping bitterly. Realizing the gravity of the situation, Cheriyatti said, "Amma, the family should not be disgraced. The land must not be reduced to rack and ruin."

The Kanancheri karanavar's anger subsided. He looked at the others around him and heaved a sigh of relief.

The nattukoottam assembled under the twin banyan trees the next day. No one from the Kanancheri tarawad went to the meeting. However, one of Atti's brothers, spurred by curiosity, went and stood

---

Karanavar: The head of a tarawad – the seniormost ammaman (uncle).

a short distance away from the assembly, pretending to look at the bamboos in the paddy field. But they spoke very softly, and although he strained his ears, he could hear nothing.

"Why not build a little hut for her somewhere behind the house far away from the tarawad precincts?" suggested one of the younger men of the family. The karanavar did not respond.

When Atti was consulted by a cousin, she muttered through her sobs, "But my sister, that doesn't remove the stigma."

The karanavar cried out in lamentation, "Oh, the spirits of my forefathers, my dead karanavars, don't subject me to this trial."

Then he narrated the story of Cheriyatti, right from the days of Atti's fasting and praying. At the end of it all, he plaintively asked his ancestors, "Oh, why should this have happened to my darling child, who not long ago played in this very courtyard, wearing her gold chain and the consecrated thread round her tender waist!"

Cheriyatti's voice was then heard.

"I will shift to the uralppura," she announced. Her eyes dazzled like lightning in the darkness of the room. Her entire body glowed, and she thrilled to a strange sensation.

"But the disgrace! It won't end with that either, my child ..." Atti diffidently reminded her.

"Kanancheri Cheriyatti doesn't need anybody's advice. She knows how to safeguard the honour of her family," she stated.

"Oh Mother, Maha Maya! Protector of the destitute ..."

As soon as the nattukoottam heard about this, the whole community buzzed with excitement. People thronged to see Cheriyatti seated cross-legged on a rough blanket in the uralppura. As if absorbed in some beautiful dream, the maiden was oblivious of the crowd before her. Seeing the radiance on her face the people folded their hands in prayer and bowed to her.

"This spot, where this Devi is now seated, before her great sukritam, will henceforth be known as the Uralppura temple. It's

---

Uralppura: A room away from the main house, for pounding grain in an ural or wooden mortar.

only after paying their obeisance here that the worshippers will go to the temple down the hill," declared Aromanejaman who had trudged with great difficulty to see Cheriyatti in this posture.

The news of Cheriyatti's divinity spread far and wide and people from the neighbouring desams hurried towards the Kanancheri uralppura.

"The night of the fourth day is auspicious for the ceremony," said Aromanejaman, after protracted calculations. "The time after Moolam when Avittam starts."

It was her mother who conveyed this decision to Cheriyatti. As she turned to go, the girl called her back and said, "Amma, please tell Valiyammaman not to have it done in the temple pond. For three or four days after that, the people will have problems bathing there."

The nattukoottam deliberated over this matter and decided on Kummanikkulam, the pond used only by the untouchables and the cattle.

The leader of the nattukoottam enquired, "Will Kothan deliver everything on time?" And then, with a sense of great pride and self-righteous indignation, he said, "The neighbouring desams may have forgotten the age-old rituals. Our ruler may not be with us, but we haven't given up our customs. What people now do is resort to deception. They remain outside of the tarawad for a certain length of time, then enter the house at the auspicious moment. What new fangled practices! I wonder what will happen to us at this rate? Certainly it was not without reason that our old karanavars laid down these rules. As long as I'm alive, things will be done as they should be. After that ... I can't imagine the state of affairs."

He heaved a deep sigh of regret.

"But what about the weeds in Kummanikkulam? Suppose the legs get entangled in them and the head resurfaces?" someone asked.

"Weren't you there when Aromanejaman said that nothing untoward should mar the event? Remember it is after many years that such a day has dawned, an occasion to perform such an auspicious deed. And that too by the flower of the Kanancheri tarawad!"

Down came some able-bodied men, promptly jumped into the pond. They took out all the tangles of moss lying at the bottom.

Aromanejaman was being given a blow by blow account of what was happening. His niece, half concealed by the door, said very humbly, "Had it not been so late at night we could have watched it too."

"No. The womenfolk cannot go to see it! After all there are certain restrictions," the old man reprimanded her. She passed on whatever she had heard to the women in the neighbouring tarawads.

All the people of the desam had to observe a fast that night. After the midday meal, the women were to engage themselves in prayer. This had been the custom since time immemorial.

❦

In the early hours of that morning, the stonecutter and his wife had delivered two granite blocks with holes cut in the centre. As remuneration for this service, he was entitled to a measure of rice and a pair of woven towels from the Kanancheri tarawad every year for the rest of his life. And the nattukoottam gave him a word of praise for the neat way in which the holes were cut.

As the time for the auspicious moment drew near, Cheriyatti was ceremoniously prepared by two pinatis – retainers, whose food and clothes were paid for by the tarawad. Except for Cheriyatti's earrings they removed all her other ornaments and handed them over to her mother. A Nair, whose privilege it was to carry the lamp, walked in front. Atti stood gazing at her daughter in the light of the lamp. Cheriyatti stepped down to the courtyard. Her eyes wore an expression of pride and dignity. The menfolk started following Cheriyatti who walked behind the lamp bearer.

Around the Kummanikkulam had gathered men of all ages – barring the very young. Anyone who could walk or limp was there. Many of them carried lamps and torches.

"Where's the rope? Who had undertaken to bring it?" asked a voice.

"It's got lost in the crowd," shouted the leader of the nattukoottam.

Cheriyatti stood on the bank, in a clearing of wild pandanus plants.

"Where's Aromanejaman?"

"I wasn't there on the last such occasion. According to the sastras, who is to tie the rope around the ankles?"

Some said it was the chief of the nattukoottam. Or was it the karanavar of the Kanancheri tarawad?

One of them, who had a sense of humour, said, "Let it be the karanavar himself, for isn't he a member of the nattukoottam as well? In that case no one can say later that rules were violated."

Slip knots were made at the end of the two ropes tied to the two slabs of stones. The karanavar said to Cheriyatti, "Child, stand with your feet inside the loops."

She did as she was bidden. While the slip knots were being tightened, the karanavar said, "Don't be afraid, there's nothing to fear. It's not the old Kummanikkulam. All the muck has been removed."

Some of the youngsters were getting impatient.

"Why is the karanavar not tightening the knots?"

"If this old man can't do it, one of you can. He only needs to touch it."

However, such an exigency did not arise. The karanavar stood aside after he had carried out his task.

Cheriyatti, who was standing alone, looked around at all the spectators. The Nair in charge of the lamp brightened its wick and, as the light fell upon her face, the people observed a smile of supreme satisfaction.

"The timid ones sometimes have to be prompted. Do you think we will need to do that?" asked a man in the crowd.

No, there was no need for that at all. Cheriyatti gazed at the crowd with her shining eyes, as if anointing and blessing them, then jumped into the pond.

For a brief moment there was utter silence. Then the people dispersed, thankful that no inauspicious happening had marred the sacred act.

❦

The nattukoottam also dispersed after deciding to return in the early hours of the next morning – by which time the water would have settled – to perform the rest of the rites.

That night, not only the Kanancheri karanavar but also all the other worthies of the place had the same strange dream: A fierce looking hunter, clad in elephant skin, wearing a chain of skulls around his neck and carrying a shining axe and a rope, suddenly descended from the skies and plunged into the Kummanikkulam waters. Then he rose and leaped back to the skies he had come from.

The nattukoottam, on reaching the banks of the Kummanikkulam early next morning, did not utter a word about the dream to one another. The untouchables, who were assigned the task of taking out the dead body, found, to their surprise, that it was not there.

The Kanancheri karanavar knew that it was a futile exercise. "That's enough." he said. "It won't be found."

The head of the nattukoottam turned to the pond and prayed. He muttered, "Sukritam! Mahasukritam!" And then said impatiently, "Come on, now. We have to discuss matters pertaining to the building of the temple. Hurry up."

The nattukoottam followed their leader to the shade of the twin banyan trees. They were in high spirits. As if renewing their memory of the dream, in one voice they exclaimed, "Amme, Bhagavati!"

A STORY IS BORN

translated by
Vanajam Ravindran

The entire story is what you, as the writer, should envisage – the characters in the story, their conversation, their feelings and emotions. You should also think of the form of the story and the fusion of its various elements. By the time you tie up the loose ends, untie them again, think over them, you have a complete idea of the story you want to write – the beginning and, sometimes, even the end.

Once the germ of the story has developed to this stage, you can set it down on paper any time. While writing out a story that has already been written in your minds, you may be confronted with altogether unexpected ideas. Later you will realize that they are congenial to the story's growth, for these portions, which are the result of sudden prompting, coalesce into the planned story and shine with a special glow. There are times when the idea of a story appears to you like a vaguely shining light. But the imaginative and mental process involved in nurturing it may not lend itself to the writer's intention or convenience. No common or universal rule can be observed as far as story writing is concerned.

❦

I think I must have written over a hundred stories – good, bad, indifferent. But it was after writing one particular story – "In Your Memory" – that I really shed tears. I cannot analyze with any clarity its gradual evolution as a story. But I clearly remember the pain and anguish I felt when I completed it.

I have no sisters. As a child I felt very deprived on this score. How I yearned for a sister!

When I was about ten, my father returned to our village after four years in Ceylon. The entire household – my mother, brothers and I – had eagerly looked forward to his arrival. He finally came, accompanied by a fair girl who could speak only Sinhalese.

The moment the girl crossed the threshold, the whole house, which had been throbbing with excitement a moment earlier, suddenly froze into a numb silence punctuated by whisperings and suspicious glances. Some said that my father had brought back with him the child of a friend who was killed in a bomb blast. What was the truth? To this day I am ignorant of the truth.

At that time, I was inclined to believe that she was my father's daughter. She had to be that, for then I would have a sister of my own. I alone was happy in the midst of the upheaval she had caused, loud alterations, accusations, tears and words of consolation. After a few days she went back with my father. For quite some time I

This is an extract from the essay, "Oru Katha Janikunnu," first published in Malayalam in *MT,* edited by V R Sudeesh, Mulberry, 1995.

could not stop thinking of her. But with time her memory gradually faded.

In June, 1954, someone told me in hushed tones, that the girl from Ceylon had got married.We were on our way to a wedding. As I walked along the crowded road full of the smell of tobacco and ringing with talk – a mixture of Malayalam and Tamil – the dim picture of a fair girl seated on an iron trunk emerged from behind the curtain of memory. I left the wedding house, perturbed. That is when I decided to write a story about her arrival at our home.

The old events and all their associations came back to me with utter clarity. If I were to write the story, my mother would have to be one of the characters. She had died just the previous year and thoughts of her made my heart heavy ... However I felt an immediate compulsion to write.

I could visualize that night of confrontations and altercations. All I needed to do was tie up the various images hovering around that scene – the visitors seated in the verandah, our newly acquired gramophone blaring on one side, the words exploding between my father and mother in the room upstairs. And in the room downstairs, a stunned and bewildered girl sitting on an iron trunk, twirling the key on her finger .

The climax could be manipulated from that scene. The story beginning with my father's arrival should end with his leaving the house. The characters – my father, my mother and the Sinhalese girl. Then a thought struck me as I sat down to write: What I am going to write is something my family has chosen to forget. Suppose my father were to read the story? I was unnerved. As it is, I was often accused of exposing my friends and relatives in my writing.

Perhaps I could present the story in another way. I made it the story of some other family – a husband, wife and a strange girl, supposedly the husband's daughter. I tried to create a setting, the right atmosphere for these people. But I tore up whatever I had written. The wild imaginings of a suspicious wife is a hackneyed theme. In the course of time I forgot all about this story.

One night, however, all the old scenes, remembered and imagined, appeared before my eyes. I was so perturbed that I got out of bed and began to write. I decided not to conceal anything. I was no longer nervous about how people would react to the story. My main problem was deciding whose perspective the story should be told from. The easiest thing would have been to narrate it in the third person. But that stance would not be suitable for a story in which the incidents are not as important as the emotions of the characters. The story had to be told from the point of view of a particular character. The Sinhalese girl could be the focal point. But, being totally ignorant of her mental makeup and background, I felt incompetent to narrate the story through her. My mother's could be an important point of view. She who had prayed and fasted and visited temples for the birth of a baby girl is shocked at the sight of a strange girl entering the house with my father. Then his perspective – pulled by love in two directions – had a lot of narrative potential too.

But suppose "I" became the narrator. I could see him clearly: A bewildered little ten-year-old boy in red shorts in the midst of a domestic furore. He is overjoyed by the arrival of a sister, but is sad when he sees the upheaval caused by her coming. He is too scared to go up and talk to her. Anyway he can't understand the language she speaks in. He can only admire her from a distance, in the nice, sweet-smelling frock she is wearing, while he is in his dirt-stained shorts. I could even hear his heartbeats. The story could be presented through his eyes. I could adopt a style suitable for rendering the responses of an innocent ten-year-old child. If I were to present it as "reminiscences," perhaps I would have at my service the language of the emotions – explosive, swirling, burning. But I was averse to this mode of writing. It would not be natural as a little boy.

I put down the date and, gazing at the past, began to write the story. The first sentence on the paper was something like this:

"After many years I suddenly remembered Leela. It is her wedding tomorrow."

When I wrote at the end, "My blessings to you, dear sister, from this far away land," my eyes welled up with tears. The original title, "A Leaf from my Life," was changed to "In Your Memory" when it was published.

That night, when I finished the story and lay down to sleep, I felt the coolness of moonlight in my heart. The story, which had caused me the utmost pain during its gestation period, was finally born.

The Crafting Years

1934 Born at Kudallur village in Palghat, Kerala.

1949 He begins contributing to periodicals.

1952 The first collection of his short stories is published.

1953 He completes his graduation from Victoria College, Palghat.

1956 He joins *Mathrubhumi,* the Malayalam magazine.

1959 The Kerala Sahitya Akademi Award is conferred on him for the novel *Nalukettu.*

1963 He travels in the USSR.

1968 He is made the editor of the *Mathrubhumi Weekly.*

1970 His novel, *Kalam,* receives the Sahitya Akademi Award.

1971 He is in the USA on a travel grant.

1973 The President's Gold Medal is awarded to the film *Nirmalyam* – written, produced and directed by him.

1974 He travels in the USSR, Europe and the Far East.

1978 The Kerala Sahitya Akademi Award is presented to MT for his play, *Gopuranatayil.*

1981 He is honoured with the Kerala Sahitya Akademi Award for his short story collection *Swargam Turakkunna Samayam.*

1984 His novel, *Randamoozham,* wins the Vayalar Award.

1989 The National Award for Best Screenplay is conferred on him for *Oru Vadakkan Veera Gatha.* He rejoins the Mathrubhumi Group of Publications as the Editor.

1992 He receives the Katha Award for Creative Fiction for the story "Cheriya Cheriya Bhookambangal."

1993 *Vanaprastham,* a collection of short stories is selected for the Otakkuzal (Mahakavi G Sankara Kurup Memorial) Award.

1996 MT receives the Jnanpith Award.

The Contributors

❦ **Anjali Singh** has studied Political Science at Lady Shri Ram College and Jawaharlal University. A research scholar, she has an MPhil in International Relations and is working for a PhD in "American Policy."

❦ **Ashutosh Roy** works with Parsec Technologies, a communication software startup. He claims to have designed and developed software, but struggles with word processors. He is convinced that some day literature can be translated by "thinking" computers. Until then, his hobby remains secure.

❦ **Babli Moitra Saraf** teaches English at Ramjas College in Delhi. After completing an advanced course in Italian at Perugia as part of an Indo-ItalianCultural Exchange Programme, she has co-translated Mahasveta Devi's *Operation Boshai Tudu* into Italian *(La Cattura,* Theoria Roma, 1996). A gifted linguist, she is fluent in Bangla, Hindi, Urdu, English and Italian.

❦ **Enakshi Chatterjee** is a writer, translator and media critic. She has translated a wide range of Bangla novels and has written over thirty books on science and science fiction for adults and children. *Paramanu Jignasa*, a book on Atomic Science, written jointly with her husband, won her the 1983 Rabindra Puroshkar from the Government of West Bengal. She lives in Calcutta.

❦ **Frederica Oddera,** a professional translator, teaches at the Italian Cultural Centre, New Delhi. She has worked with leading Italian publishing houses like Mondadari and knows French, English, German and Italian. Frederica, with Babli, has translated Mahasveta Devi's *Operation Boshai Tudu* into Italian.

❦ **Ganesh Devy** is Professor of English at the Maharaja Sayajirao University at Baroda. He translates from Marathi and Gujarati into English and was the recipient of the Katha Award for Translation (1992). He has been the editor of SETU, a journal of translation in Gujarati and English. He has held many distinguished fellowships including the Commonwealth Academic Staff Fellowship, the Fulbright Fellowship, the T H B Symons Fellowship and the Jawaharlal Nehru Fellowship. He has been a Visiting Professor at Yale University, and he received the Sahitya Akademi Award in 1993 for his book, *After Amnesia: Change in Literary Criticism*.

- **Geeta Dharmarajan** is a writer for children and adults. Editor of the *Katha Prize Stories*, an annual anthology of the best of Indian regional fiction in translation, Geeta also writes and edits *Tamasha!* – a fun and activity magazine on development issues for first generation school-goers. She started Katha in 1988 and is its Executive Director.

- **H Y Sharada Prasad** was Information Adviser to Prime Minister Rajiv Gandhi. He has translated two of K Shivarama Karanth's novels and his autobiography into English, and R K Narayan's *Swami and Friends* into Kannada. He received the Katha Award for Translation in 1994..

- **Jayeeta Sharma** is a research scholar in the field of Modern Indian History. She is currently teaching at Lady Shri Ram College in Delhi. She translates from Assamese to English and has won the Katha Award for Translation in 1994.

- **Lalita Vivekanand** has a postgraduate diploma in book publishing, and certificates in Education and Food Preservation and Nutrition. She has travelled widely and taught in schools and colleges all over the world. With many publications to her credit, Lalita has just finished work on a history of Kannada literature, to be published by Ratna Sagar, New Delhi.

- **Meenakshi Sharma** studied English at Lady Shri Ram College, Delhi. She has co-edited *Katha Prize Stories Volume 5*, and works at Katha.

- **Mridula Nath Chakraborty** is an MPhil in English from Delhi University. She is interested in 19th century world literature, traditional Indian recipes and Kishore Kumar memorabilia.

- **Naushil Mehta**, a graduate in Chemistry, is a successful playwright and a writer of short fiction. He has also directed a number of plays. He lives in Bombay and is now working on a long short story.

- **Prasanna** is a playright, director and designer. He passed out of NSD with distinction for a diploma in direction in 1975. Between 1975 and 1982, he mobilized a mass cultural movement spearheading the campaign for radical mass education. He has been awarded by the Karnataka Sahitya Akademi and the Sangeet Natak Akademi. He stays in Heggodu, Karnataka.

- **Rajan Chakraborty** has an MA in Political Science and has worked for *The Statesman*, *Sunday Observer* and *Delhi Mid-day*. He is now a freelance journalist and an aspiring writer. Cricket and cinema are his passions – so by default he is consumed by television.

- **Tarun Bhartiya** has dabbled in politics, published poetry, made videos, directed plays and studied Economics and Mass Communication. An editor with New Delhi Television, his other major preoccupation is cooking.

- **Upendra Nanavati** is a reader in English at MS University, Baroda. His area of specialization is Indian criticism in English, Gujarati and Marathi. He received the Katha Award for Translation in 1995.

- **Vanajam Ravindran** retired as reader in English from Lady Shri Ram College, University of Delhi. She has published occasional articles, translations and book-reviews in journals. She is now editing a collection of Vaikom Muhammad Basheer's stories for Katha.

Photo Credits

Sahitya Akademi: for the photographs of U R Anantha Murthy on the contents page and page 11; of Mahasveta Devi on the contents page and page 159; of M T Vasudevan Nair on pages 197 and 202.

***Outlook*:** for the photographs of Bhupen Khakhar on pages 63 and 68 (Prashant Panjiar); of Krishna Sobti on page 104 (Jitender Gupta).

Babli Moitra Saraf: for the photograph of Mahasveta Devi on page 164.

Bhupen Khakhar: for his photograph on the Contents page.

Krishna Sobti: for her photographs on the contents page and page 99.

Katha: for the photograph of U R Anantha Murthy on page 16.

About Katha

KATHA is a registered nonprofit organization devoted to creative communication for development. Katha's basic objective is to spread the love of books and the joy of reading amongst children and adults. Our activities span from literacy to literature.

KALPAVRIKSHAM, Katha's Centre for Sustainable Learning, develops and publishes quality material for neo-literate children and adults, and works with teachers to help them make their teaching and presentation more creative. The publications for first-generation schoolgoers and adult neo-literates are learning packages, specially designed for use in nonformal education –*Hulgul ka Pitara,* a basic Hindi language package. In the making is *Chaand!*, an integrated kit for the teaching of science, mathematics and language to pre-schoolers. And, every quarter, Katha brings out *Tamasha!,* a fun and activity magazine on development issues for children in Hindi and English. The *Katha Vachak* series is an attempt to take fiction to neo-literates, especially women. It also includes *Stree Katha,* a beautifully illustrated, information-packed, interactive book on women's issues.

THE KHAZANA EXPERIMENT, a part of Kalpavriksham, was started in 1990 in one of Delhi's largest slum cluster, in Govindpuri. Kathashala and the Katha School of Entrepreneurship have about 1000 students – mostly working children. To enhance their futures, an income-generation programme for the women of this community – Shakti-Khazana – and the Khazana Women's Cooperative were also started here, in 1990.

KATHA VILASAM is the Story Research And Resource Centre of Katha. It seeks to foster and applaud the best short fiction from the regional languages and take it to a wider readership through translations. The Katha Awards, instituted in 1990, are given annually to the best short fiction published in the regional languages that year, and for translations of these stories. Through projects like the Translation Contest, it attempts to build up a bank of sensitive translators. In addition to this, Katha Vilasam functions as a literary agency and works with academia to associate students in translation-related activities. KathaNet, an invaluable network of Friends of Katha, is the mainstay of all Katha Vilasam efforts.

YuvaKatha is a series for the young adult. *A Unique Odyssey: The Story of the UN,* an exciting fusion of fantasy and reality, was the first book in the series, which also includes a set of twelve slim volumes of the best of Indian short fiction. Katha has recently launched the BalKatha series for younger children with *The Secrets of Kalindi: A Jigsaw Puzzle Adventure*.